• HALSGROVE DISCOVER SERIES ➤

SHAKESPEARE COUNTRY: WARWICKSHIRE

Robin Jones

HALSGROVE

First published in Great Britain in 2010

British Library Cataloguing-in-Publication Data
A CIP record for this title is available from the British Library

ISBN 978 1 84114 932 5

HALSGROVE
Halsgrove House,
Ryelands Industrial Estate,
Bagley Road, Wellington, Somerset TA21 9PZ
Tel: 01823 653777 Fax: 01823 216796
email: sales@halsgrove.com

Part of the Halsgrove group of companies
Information on all Halsgrove titles is available at: www.halsgrove.com

Printed and bound in China by Toppan Leefung Printing Ltd

To my brother Stewart,
who showed me much of old Arden by
bicycle when I was very young

CONTENTS

The birthplace of William Shakespeare in Henley Street, Stratford-upon-Avon.

The historic county of Warwickshire included Coventry, Solihull and much of Birmingham. All three became part of the metropolitan county of the West Midlands following local government reorganisation in 1974, but this county was in turn abolished in 1986 except for ceremonial purposes, with the three becoming authorities outside of modern Warwickshire. But in the greater sweep of history, and certainly as Shakespeare would have known his home county, these settlements were in Warwickshire and covered by the Forest of Arden which extended over the centre and north of the county. For the purposes of this book they are treated, therefore, as part of Warwickshire.

1

FOREST OF DREAMS AND DELIGHT

Weaving ancient woodland magic

Over hill, over dale,
Through bush, through briar,
Over park, over pale,
Through flood, through fire,
I do wander everywhere,
Swifter than the moon's sphere;
And I serve the fairy queen,
To dew her orbs upon the green.
The cowslips tall her pensioners be:
In their gold coats, spots you see;
Those be rubies, fairy favours,
In those freckles live their savours:
I must go seek some dewdrops here
And hang a pearl in every cowslip's ear.
Farewell, thou lob of spirits; I'll be gone:
Our queen and all our elves come here anon.
(A Midsummer Night's Dream, Act 2, Scene 1)

Shakespeare Country and Warwickshire, with the ancient Forest of Arden covering much of its central and northern lands, are forever intertwined. The Bard was descended from the old Arden family who took their name from the great prehistoric woodland on the doorstep of his boyhood home, and which became a major source of inspiration in at least two of his plays.

Despite a popular misconception, there is far more to Arden than Shakespeare and Stratford-upon-Avon, even though the great forest was cleared centuries ago, leaving just occasional pockets of woodland and a multitude of magnificent half-timbered houses built from local oaks.

The cover of the first folio of 1623.

Narrow winding Roman Icknield Street, seen near Weatheroak Hill, forms the western boundary of Arden.

Yes, Shakespeare was by far the most famous, but he was certainly not the only artist nurtured by the Forest of Arden, and on our travels in this volume we will meet many others, from Lord of the Rings creator J.R.R. Tolkein, who was certainly inspired by the sylvan rural landscape of the northern edges of the forest, to the man who wrote *It's A Long Way to Tipperary* and a lost musical genius of the late sixties.

In the absence of a sizeable spread of woodland today, many inevitably ask – where exactly is the Forest of Arden?

Historians have given its boundaries as the River Avon to the south, the Roman road Icknield (or Ryknield Street) to the west, the River Tame to the north and the Fosse Way to the east. Much of this area has since been swallowed up by the urban sprawls of Birmingham/Solihull and Coventry/Nuneaton, and so this book will primarily focus on the core of old Arden, with Henley-in-Arden its historic heart.

The Warwickshire historian William Dugdale described the Avon as dividing the "wooded part" of the county from the Feldon, the southern 'half' which became fields centuries earlier. The heavy clay soil of Arden was less susceptible to clearance for farmland: dig nine inches down, and you will hit a bed of clay, of which oaks, the principal tree of Arden, thrive.

Arden was settled long before the Romans. Early settlers encountered a barely-penetrable almost Amazonian green woody mass spreading across the heights of the Midland plateau.

Old Stone Age axes were found around Coventry, and New Stone Age long barrows and pottery near Warwick.

By Iron Age times, organised settlements were linked by trackways through the forest. Berry Mound, an 11-acre Iron Age village with banks and ditches overlooking the River Cole at Majors Green near Shirley, survives as an earthwork.

Arden's eastern side: leafy Kenilworth Road, Coventry, in Edwardian times.

Two thousands years ago, oak trees covered most of Warwickshire north of the River Avon.

The Romans built roads around the forest, not through it, and as in later centuries, it would have been a great refuge from those seeking to avoid the law.

The major settlement of Arden began between the seventh and tenth centuries, by two groups of Germanic settlers, the Angles and the Saxons from the south, some journeying from the North Sea along rivers like the Tame and the Blythe.

They created small clearings for settlements. The names of many Arden villages end with 'ley' or 'leigh', a Saxon suffix meaning 'woodland clearing'.

Examples are Baddesley-Clinton (leah owned by Clinton), Bentley Heath, Solihull (bent grass leah), Crackley Wood near Coventry, Haseley (hazel leah), Honiley (honey leah), Shelley (leah on slope), Shrewley (sheriff's leah), Stoneleigh (stony leah) and Studley (pasture for horses).

The name Arden comes from the British Celtic 'ard' meaning high, and 'denu' a valley, like the Forest of Ardennes in France and Belgium.

Arden became part of the kingdom of Mercia. The mighty Arden family descended from Aelfwine an Anglo-Saxon nobleman who was sheriff of Warwickshire in 1050, and may have been descended from Mercian kings and related to Lady Godiva.

Aelfwine's son, Thurkill, was one of only two Saxon noblemen in England whose lands were not seized by William the Conqueror.

Thurkill did not attend the Battle of Hastings, and so greatly pleased William.

Under orders from William he constructed a ditch with an entrance gate around the town of Warwick. Thurkill became known as the Traitor Earl, but his family still held many of the same manors in Shakespeare's day.

When surnames were introduced as an aid to poll tax, Thurkill took the name of de Arden after the forest. The first recorded spelling of the family name is that of Thurkill de Arden in the *Domesday Book* of 1086, and five centuries later, the best-known member of the family was born . . . Mary Arden.

There was, however, a darker and deeper side to the forest, which embodied a much older and mystical order refuted by the 'modern' world, where nature, not man, set the standards – and Shakespeare knew it.

It was the great forest in which his ancestors had lived, and in turn provided the settings for *As You Like It* and *A Midsummer Night's Dream*.

As You Like It sees Duke Senior usurped by his wicked younger brother, Duke Frederick – and where does he take refuge with his companions? In the Forest of Arden: '*They say he is already in the forest of Arden, and a many merry men with him; and there they live like the old Robin Hood of England: they say many young gentlemen flock to him every day, and fleet the time carelessly, as they did in the golden world.*'

Orlando, the youngest of three sons of the late Sir Rowland de Boys, also flees to the forest after falling in love with Rosalind, cousin to Celia, the only child of Duke Frederick, who discovers Orlando is his old enemy's son. The livid Frederick banishes Rosalind, who, along with Celia, enters the forest in

Warwickshire's emblem of a bear and ragged staff, seen at Berkswell's Bear Inn, was also that of Thurkell of Warwick, founder of the Arden family.

Beefsteak fungus (fistulina hepatica) is an oak parasite which softens the wood and turns it a rich reddish brown, highly valued in the furniture trade.

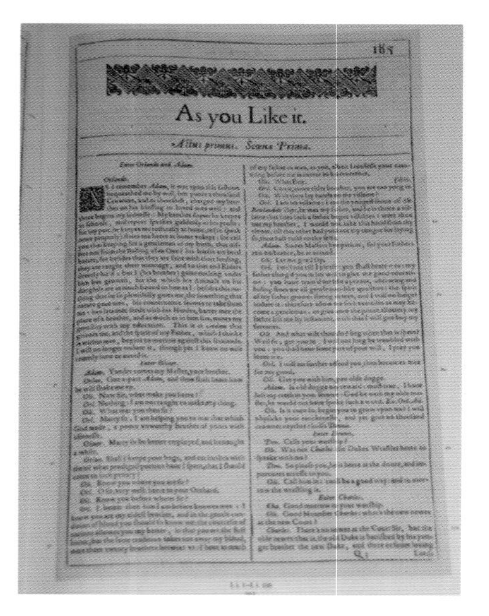
185

As you Like it.

Actus primus. Scena Prima.

The first folio opening page of As You Like It.

search of Duke Senior, taking along Frederick's jester, Touchstone. In the forest, the girls undergo a strange transformation: Rosalind disguises herself as a boy called Ganymede, while Celia adopts "poor and mean attire" and takes the name Aliena.

In disguise, Rosalind meets Orlando, and pretends she is a boy in turn pretending to be Rosalind! Typical figures from the literary tradition of the pastoral, in which rural life is idealised, appear. Phebe, a shepherdess, falls in love with Ganymede, in turn leaving shepherd Silvius heartbroken, while Touchstone declares his love for Audrey, a goatherd, who in turn is loved by William, a simple countryman.

Celia, meanwhile, collects love poems which Orlando has written to Rosalind and pinned on trees all over the forest.

Eventually, thanks to the magical power of the forest, natural harmony is restored from human chaos, and those banished can return in happiness and safety to the court.

In the chapters that follow, we will see how, during the reign of the protestant Elizabeth I, the forest became a major bolthole for those who stayed Catholic, and who may have included Shakespeare's own family, all but secure from the shadow of the Tower of London and the unpleasantness that awaited offenders within its soundproof and unforgiving walls.

Just as Arden offered a means of escape back into old ways from the corrupted power of the contemporary court of England and the society it ruled, so the forest of the play offers freedom, a

The undisputed lord of the forest in Packington Park.

The Stratford-upon-Avon Canal near Earlswood in autumn.

The nineteenth-century fingerpost road sign in Norton Lindsey.

dream world in which time stands still and hidden forces unleash their supernatural healing processes.

Shakespeare contrasted the simplicity of forest life with the artificial manners and hypocrisy of the court. Duke Senior tells his companions:

Now, my co-mates and brothers in exile,
Hath not old custom made this life more sweet
Than that of painted pomp? Are not these woods
More free from peril than the envious court?
Here feel we but the penalty of Adam,
The seasons' difference, as the icy fang
And churlish chiding of the winter's wind,
Which, when it bites and blows upon my body,
Even till I shrink with cold, I smile and say
'This is no flattery: these are counsellors
That feelingly persuade me what I am.'
Sweet are the uses of adversity,
Which, like the toad, ugly and venomous,
Wears yet a precious jewel in his head;
And this our life exempt from public haunt
Finds tongues in trees, books in the running brooks,
Sermons in stones and good in every thing.
I would not change it.

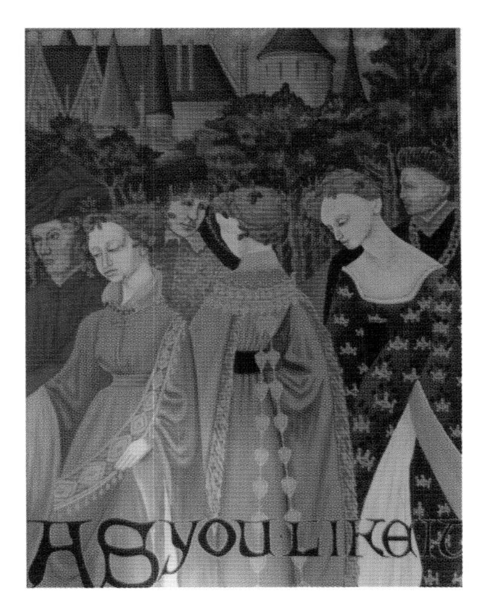

A vintage poster for As You Like It, *Shakespeare's comedy set in Arden.*

This is also the realm of pre-Christian beliefs, paganism and wicca, forgotten knowledge supposedly subjugated by the modern faith, yet which still lurked deep within the human consciousness.

The image of the greenwood manifests itself as the Green Knight in the Arthurian legends; the Green Man, a pre-Christian symbol of the natural order allied with humanity, the wood demon Jack-in-the Green, and the legends of Robin Hood – and his merrie men of the greenwood:

Under the greenwood tree
Who loves to lie with me,
And turn his merry note
Unto the sweet bird's throat,
Come hither, come hither, come hither:
Here shall he see No enemy
But winter and rough weather.
(*As You Like It*, Act 2, Scene 5).

The happy forest reunion of Rosalind, her father Duke Senior and lover Orlando in As You Like It.

Right: *The hapless Bottom has turned into an ass, with Titania's fairies depicted as frightening creatures of the forest, during a Stamford Shakespeare Company production of* A Midsummer Night's Dream.

Far right: *Arden fantasy: Puck and a fairy deep in discussion during a Stamford Shakespeare Company production of* A Midsummer Night's Dream *at Tolethorpe open-air theatre in Lincolnshire.*

One question often asked is – was the Arden of *As You Like It* in Warwickshire, or like several of Shakespeare's plays, set on the continent? The story of Rosalind and Orlando came from Thomas Lodge's *Rosalynde*, which was set in the Ardennes. However, the great thick green canopy of Warwickshire would have served Shakespeare well as a literary device, and one with which he was familiar.

Every fairytale needs a forest – *Snow White, Little Red Riding Hood, Hansel and Gretel, Robin Hood* – and *A Midsummer Night's Dream* is no exception.

The play's forest is a leafy domain stretching without end, in which wild animals and mythical figures again magically appear. Once more, the lovers belong in the outside world, that of the court, but come to 'find' themselves and their true feelings for each other only in the forest.

Sadly, the real Arden awoke from its dream four centuries ago, when the slow process of deforestation accelerated.

The Elizabethans were only too aware of the loss of their woodland: the poet Michael Drayton longed for times when "this whole country's face was forestry."

Snowbound Dyer's Lane in Illshaw Heath near Earlswood, its mighty Arden oaks laid bare.

A typical cottage built with Arden oaks at Bearley near Stratford-upon-Avon.

It is 1 January 2000, and the dawn of a new millennium breaks over Light Hall Farm in Dog Kennel Lane, Shirley.

Population growth led to the need for more farmland for crops, and the Industrial Revolution demanded timber for its furnaces. By the mid-nineteenth century only two million acres of woodland were left in England and Wales.

Yet the greenwood has never entirely vanished from Arden.

Drive through the region with its gently-rolling pastures, experience the endless winding lanes and ancient hedgerows fringed by mature trees, and delight upon the quaintly-named immaculate villages that grew up in the clearings and which Shakespeare would have known.

There is a unique charm to this part of old Warwickshire that has never allowed itself to die, and hopefully never will.

In ensuing chapters, we will, like the early settlers, follow Arden's two principal rivers, the Alne and the Blythe, to begin our discovery of Shakespeare's forest.

Old Arden, as seen from Bowles' New Medium Map of Warwickshire, published on 3 January 1785.

Henley-in-Arden's famous ice cream parlour.

2

DOWN THE ALNE TO ARDEN'S CAPITAL

Tanworth-in-Arden, Umberslade, Henley-in-Arden

Under the greenwood tree
Who loves to lie with me,
And turn his merry note
Unto the sweet bird's throat,
Come hither, come hither, come hither:
Here shall he see No enemy
But winter and rough weather.
(*As You Like It*, Act 2, Scene V)

Henley-in-Arden, not as popularly believed, Stratford-upon-Avon, is the true historical capital of the Forest of Arden. However, the starting point for our step-by-step exploration will be Tanworth-in-Arden to the north.

Tanworth is not the centre of the old forest, let alone that of England. However, it includes the settlement of Wood End, which includes the great watershed of the Midlands.

Standing over 500 feet above sea level, somewhere in Wood End, a name reflecting forest origins, exists an unmarked line dividing the country. Rain falling to the north enters the valley of the River Blythe, which leads through Solihull to the Tame, and in turn the Trent, Humber and North Sea. Rainfall to the south of this line drains into the River Alne, and via the Arrow, Avon, Severn and Bristol Channel, ends up in the Atlantic Ocean. A great divide indeed for such a humble spot!

Our first forest journey here concerns the upper half of the Alne, to Henley.

The ancient Britons called the river Alwine, meaning 'clear' and 'bright'. It was first recorded around 730 as Aeluuinne, or very white.'

Its source lies in Worcestershire at the curiously-named farming hamlet of Pink Green, where run-off from fields into ditches forms the initial trickle.

Pink Green, the source of the River Alne, whose name however means 'white'.

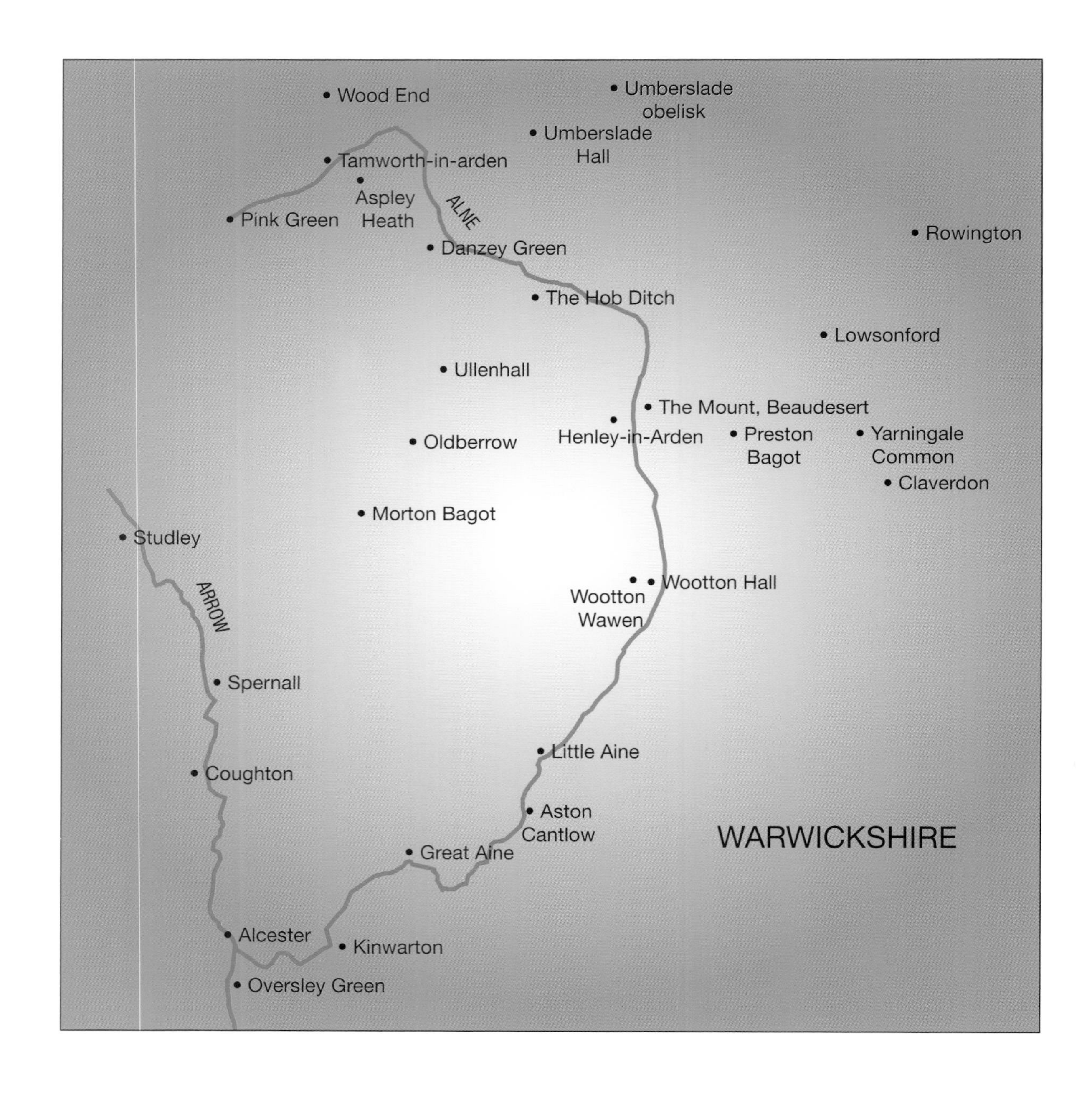
Wood End
Umberslade obelisk
Umberslade Hall
Tamworth-in-arden
Aspley Heath
Pink Green
ALNE
Danzey Green
Rowington
The Hob Ditch
Lowsonford
Ullenhall
The Mount, Beaudesert
Henley-in-Arden
Oldberrow
Preston Bagot
Yarningale Common
Claverdon
Morton Bagot
Studley
ARROW
Wootton Hall
Wootton Wawen
Spernall
Little Aine
Coughton
Aston Cantlow
Great Aine
WARWICKSHIRE
Alcester
Kinwarton
Oversley Green

The tiny stream passes beneath the A435 Alcester to Birmingham Road and leafy Alderhanger Lane to enter Tanworth parish, which straddles the watershed and also includes Earlswood.

Running south of the hamlet of Aspley Heath, the "aspen woodland clearing" added to Tanworth parish in 1895, the Alne winds around the north of Tanworth village, which occupies a strategic location on the top of a hill skirted by ancient meadows and fields.

Legends tell of mighty battles being fought in this area, and the Warwickshire antiquarian Sir William Dugdale wrote of 2000 bodies buried in a mass grave which has never been found. What has been discovered were the remains of men and horses plus swords and cannonballs near Tanworth's church of St Mary Magdalene, proof that an English Civil War skirmish took place there.

The church dates from the twelfth century, and underwent drastic alterations in 1790 by vicar the Reverend Philip Wren, great grandson of Sir Christopher Wren, architect of St Paul's Cathedral. However, the reverend showed little of the artistic vision of his famous forebear: much of the fine medieval fabric was swept away, but satisfactorily restored in 1880.

Another incumbent was Robert Chichester, Lord Moncrieff, vicar for 28 years until his death in 1913. Fed up with letters going astray to Tamworth in Staffordshire, he successfully petitioned for the village name to be changed to Tanworth-in-Arden.

Two gravestones in the churchyard are those of national figures. Ten-times world motorcycling champion Mike Hailwood and his nine-year-old daughter Michelle, who died in a road accident near Wythall in 1981, are buried there.

The village green at Tanworth-in-Arden was known as 'the roundabout.'

Look no cars! An early twentieth-century postcard view of Tanworth-in-Arden.

Nick Drake, a singer-songwriter and musician all but unknown in his day, but who since his death at the age of 26 has attracted a cult following and is regarded by many musicians as a genius, also has a memorial.

His debut album *Five Leaves Left* was released by Island Records in 1969, and he released two more LPs none of which sold more than 5000 copies at the time. Drake suffered from depression and insomnia, and in November 1974, he died from an overdose of a prescribed antidepressant.

However, by the mid-1980s, his posthumous stature had grown to such extent that major artists like Kate Bush, Paul Weller and the Dream Academy cited him as a major influence. In 2000, Volkswagen featured the title track from his last album *Pink Moon* in a TV advertisement, and within a month more Nick Drake records were sold than in the previous 30 years.

His gravestone is inscribed with the epitaph *'Now we rise/And we are everywhere'*, taken from the final song on *Pink Moon*.

Tanworth was also the filming location for the fictional village of Kings Oak in the British soap opera *Crossroads* between 1970 and 1988, which, ironically, starred Drake's sister Gabrielle.

The Saxon name Tanworth deriving from Tanewotha, 'thane's worth' or 'estate'. A thane was granted land by the king in return for military service. In 872, Waerferth, Bishop of Worcester, granted the King's thane, Eanwulf, a lease on substantial land holdings there. His name may have become transformed into Tanworth.

Tanworth was certainly a place of conflict and battle into modern times, for a former landlord of the Bell Inn which stands on the village green was Jack Hood, Britain's undefeated

The war memorial in the centre of Tanworth-in-Arden.

The Bell Inn, once run by one of Britain's greatest boxers.

welterweight boxing champion, who lost only five bouts in a 33-year career. He died in 1992 aged 89.

The Alne passes three times beneath the North Warwickshire railway line, built by the Great Western Railway and opened between Birmingham, Tyseley and Stratford-upon-Avon in 1908. Tanworth is still served by a station at the nearby hamlet of Danzey Green.

The Alne is bridged by the most unusual of the 64 bridges on the line. It is a skew bridge (built on a curve) which also crosses the historic drive to Umberslade Hall. When asked for permission to cross his land, the owner insisted that the GWR build a bridge not with iron girders but stone, to match the colour of the mansion a mile away set in its own landscaped parkland.

Umberslade Hall was built on the site of a medieval moated manor around 1680 by Andrew Archer, a descendant of Robert Sagittarius or Robert the Archer, who came over with William the Conqueror in 1066. The family went on to own most of the manor houses in Tanworth.

The owner of Umberslade Hall became Baron Archer in 1747, and perhaps to mark the honour, he built the mysterious obelisk which towers over the M40 nearby.

Umberslade subsequently passed into the hands of Birmingham MP Bolton King, who eventually sold it to the Muntz family, whose ancestors include a royalist who fled the French Revolution.

During the Second World War, the hall was occupied by troops, including contingents from occupied Belgium and Czechoslovakia.

In the sixties, the hall became the research and development section of Triumph/BSA motorcycles, housing around 300 staff. It was subsequently converted into private apartments.

The unusual skew railway bridge over the mile-long driveway to Umberslade Hall.

Baron Archer's obelisk at Umberslade.

Umbersale Hall, once home to the Archer family.

Returning to the Alne, the little river flows on through Danzey Green, which takes its name from Nicholas Densi, a landowner in 1327, when monks harvested local fishponds as an important supply of food.

A nineteenth-century post mill from Danzey Green, a type of windmill which can be turned to catch the breeze, was dismantled in 1969 and re-erected at the Avoncroft Museum of Historic Buildings near Bromsgrove, before being restored to pristine condition.

Below Danzey, the Alne encounters a mysterious earthwork, which looks every bit like a disused railway embankment. It is the Hob Ditch Causeway which, dating back at least to early Saxon times, may have been a boundary marking the territory of early settlers of this part of Arden.

The Alne has by now grown in sufficient size to power watermills, such at Botley Mill, half a mile before the Bird in Hand pub on the main Birmingham to Stratford road, now the A3400, is reached.

Hereabouts, the Alne at times of flood has been more akin to white rapids than white water. On 18 June 1872, a horse and cart were washed away near the pub. The driver escaped but the horse drowned.

Danzey Green's post mill, now at Avoncroft Museum near Bromsgrove.

Typical Arden rural scene overlooking the mysterious Hob's Ditch Causeway.

The Alne runs alongside the main road before passing through the arch of a disused railway line, which, when opened on 6 June 1894, was the first branch to Henley-in-Arden. Superseded by the North Warwickshire line which also served the town, passenger services from Lapworth (then known as Kingswood) via Rowington Junction were "temporarily" withdrawn on 1 January 1916, never to be restored. The track was lifted and sent to France for the war effort, only for the ship carrying it to be torpedoed by a German submarine.

The original Henley station, which was later connected to the North Warwickshire line on the far side of the town, was used for freight until 31 December 1962.

Beyond the arch, the Alne acts as a boundary between twin towns Beaudesert – the older and originally by far the more powerful – and Henley-in-Arden.

Many people who enchanted by Henley's superb rows of half-timbered houses and shops inevitably ask the question: "Where is Beaudesert?"

A left turning past the 'no through road' sign in the centre of Henley brings the visitor to Beaudesert Lane and the handful of cottages that occupy the site of this once-prosperous medieval town.

The Alne approaching Henley-in-Arden.

Above and right: *Beaudesert's church of St Nicholas and its Norman gateway.*

Beaudesert was founded by the de Montfort family who settled there after the Norman Conquest and named the place Beldesert, the 'beautiful waste'.

Thurstan de Montfort built a castle on top of the hill known as the Mount, which still stands sentinel over Henley, and once reigned supreme over the surrounding forest.

Thurston's typical fortified Norman motte and bailey castle was built of wood and stone, possibly on the site of an ancient British fort.

In 1140, a charter to hold a market and weekly fair in the castle was granted, making it a local centre for commerce.

Not only did Beaudesert become a boom town but Henley, on the other side of the flood-prone river, also did very well out of it and began to grow too.

Beaudesert's parish church of St Nicholas, famous for its beautiful Norman arches, was built around this time.

In 1220, Henry III granted another charter, to Peter de Montfort, to hold a weekly market and a yearly fair at the feast of St Giles. Peter was subsequently killed along with his more famous cousin Simon de Montfort, Earl of Leicester, at the Battle of Evesham on 3 August 1265, during the Barons War.

The Mount, the site of the castle at Beaudesert.

Back at Beaudesert, as revenge for Peter's part in the revolt, his castle was burned down by royalists, along with Henley.

However, Henley prospered in the wake of Beaudesert's demise, and the castle was rebuilt.

Henley grew into an important market town as part of the parish of Wootton Wawen, and by 1367, it was given its own church for the first time.

Peter de Montfort's grandson Peter died in 1369, after which the castle passed to Thomas, Earl of Warwick, who did not really need it.

He had his own much bigger and far more important seat, Warwick Castle, and paid scant attention to Beaudesert's humble keep.

Lord Bergavenny held the castle from 1376 to 1410 after which it passed to the Boteiller family of Sudeley in Gloucestershire. It was bought from them by Edward IV in 1477.

The castle dwindled in importance to the point where it was abandoned by or in the sixteenth century.

Today it looks little different to an Iron Age earthwork of a millennium before, and only one piece of stonework from the castle survives.

Henley, however, a classic example of a linear settlement, is a veritable gem among English small towns.

Its Saxon name means 'high clearing' in the forest.

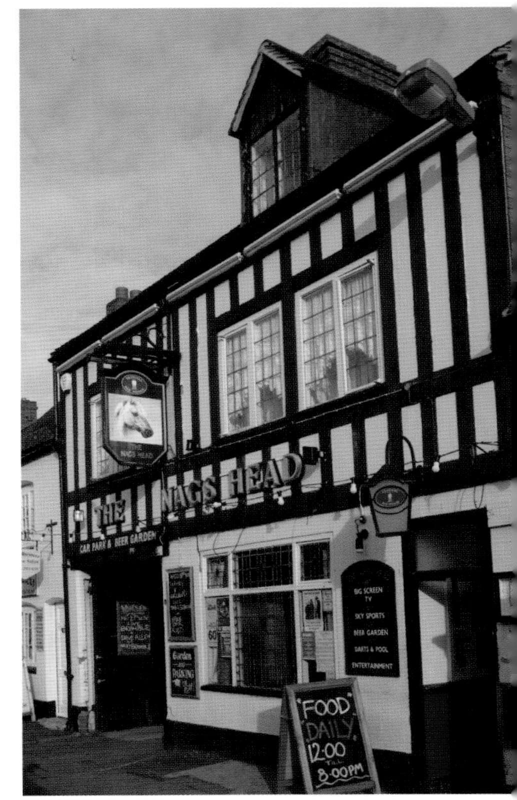

The Nag's Head, one of several traditional hostelries in Henley's High Street.

Henley's High Street in Edwardian times.

Henley's main Millennium project was this modern stained glass window in St John the Baptist church. It portrays Jesus in High Street surrounded by local children and townsfolk including a district nurse, fireman, butcher, coach driver and the town crier. The blue zig-zig represents the Alne.

A mile long, its High Street conservation area contains not only many fine half-timbered buildings constructed from Arden oaks of old, but several in later styles from the fifteenth century onwards.

While Henley, unlike Beaudesert, did not have a market charter, it was still a market town, run by a manorial court or leet, which appointed a high bailiff who would formally open the annual town fair. The leet appointed a variety of officials including a low bailiff, a third-borough, a constable, pairs of chamberlains, ale tasters, leather sealers, field reeves and, to ensure the clear passages of the Alne, brooklookers.

The Alne has also flooded Henley, often to a depth of several feet. On New Year's Eve 1899, the floods were so great that one resident, Peter Newcombe swam down High Street. In 1968, floodwaters rose a foot every 15 minutes, swamping the town and cutting off its telephones.

The leet largely handled minor problems such as livestock running loose or too many beggars entering Henley. In Shakespeare's *Love's Labours Lost*, Rosalind remarks "Better wits have worn plain Statute Caps.". This is held to refer to contemporary events in Henley when townsfolk were prosecuted in the leet for breaking a statute that required the wearing of woollen caps on Sundays and other holy days, a law introduced to boost economic support for the wool industry.

Henley suffered another misfortune during the English Civil War, when it was plundered by the royalist Prince Rupert.

In the old Market Place in High Street stands the fifteenth-century Market Cross, one of the few still existing in Warwickshire. Proclamations have been made from the cross for five centuries and the accession of Queen Elizabeth in 1952 and her jubilee in 1977 were declared there. By 1814, Henley had a weekly market every Monday, and three annual fairs, on Lady Day, on the Tuesday of Whit week for cattle and on 29 October for horses, cattle, sheep, and hops.

The Guild Hall, a half-timbered Elizabethan building next to St John's parish church, is where the court leet, which was revived in 1915, meets annually to elect its officials with traditional ceremony. A very English custom indeed, and one which has been exempted from an Act of Parliament of 1976 which swept away most other antiquated courts: however, the manor was subsequently bought by a family from the United States!

Mrs Robin Hardy-Freed, daughter of lumber millionaire Mr Joseph Hardy of Pittsburgh, Pennsylvania, became lord of the manor after he bought the title at a London auction. Hardy has since taken a great interest in Henley and paid for the Guild Cottage to be renovated and contributed towards a heritage and educational centre in High Street.

Next door to the heritage centre stands the home of Henley Ice Cream, one of the town's biggest claims to fame in the past century.

Ice creams were first made by hand here in 1890s. By the 1930s, when the business was run by Harry and Arthur Fathers, their ice creams were voted the best in Britain.

Henley was a favourite summer destination by train and omnibus for Birmingham families, and in 1937, a riot nearly broke out when hundreds of daytrippers queued outside the ice cream parlour, which was forced to buy a special uniform for an assistant to direct traffic.

Henley's historic market cross.

During the Second World War, goats milk was used to make ice cream due to shortages, and when water ran short, a diviner found an old well in the back yard.

The White Swan in High Street is one of Britain's oldest coaching inns, dating back to 1350. In its heyday before the coming of railways, seven out of 22 London to Birmingham daily stagecoaches stopped there.

Local poet William Shenstone (1714–1763) was inspired by the White Swan to write his famous lines:

Whoever has travelled life's dull round,
Wherever his stages may have been,
May sigh to think he still has found,
The warmest welcome at an inn.

The White Swan is said to be haunted by the ghost of an 18-year-old lady of the night named Virginia Black who died after falling down stairs during a quarrel with a gentleman in 1845. Also, the courtyard was at one time used for public hangings.

Staff and guests have reported seeing strange orbs, which on photographs resemble faces when magnified.

One landlord in recent times was the late *Boon* actor Michael Elphick.

Like Tanworth, Henley acquired its 'in Arden' tag due to postal mix-ups, to differentiate it from Henley-on-Thames, where mail often ended up.

The White Swan, Henley's famous old coaching inn.

The site of St John the Baptist church dates from 1367, the present structure being erected in 1448. The Guild Hall is next door.

A milestone stating Henley's place on the stagecoach route.

The Winged Spur pub in Ullenhall.

3
THE HEART OF THE FOREST

Ullenhall, Morton Bagot, Preston Bagot, Claverdon, Yarningale, Lowsonford

For those wishing to explore deepest Arden, Henley is an excellent place to begin. However, do not expect signposts to modern tourist attractions, or amenities 'laid on' for the mass market, for what awaits you will be no more or less than classic Warwickshire villages nestled in rolling countryside, without the more excessive trappings of commercialisation. Like tourists honeypots elsewhere, they are stepped in history, but you have to find it for yourself, and for many, therein lies their beauty.

Beginning their existence as forest clearings, and ancient agricultural communities in their own right, what was the historic hinterland of Henley's market is now the West Midlands stock-broker belt. Cottages built for farmworkers are now the homes of wealthy commuters, who have airbrushed them to perfection.

While Shakespeare instantly comes to mind when Warwickshire is mentioned in any artistic context, the county has been home to many other writers and artists, including an eighteenth-century literary circle which gathered around a stately home in the village of Ullenhall to the west of Henley.

Ullenhall's great mansion, Barrells Hall, was home to Henrietta, Lady Luxborough, banished there by her husband's family after an alleged affair, about which few details ever came to light.

Born around 1700, a half sister to Viscount Bolingbroke, Minister of State to Queen Anne, it was said that Henrietta was taught music by Handel.

In 1727, she married Robert Knight, son of the cashier of the South Sea Company – the very same behind the infamous South Sea Bubble. A false economic boom occurred when wild speculation sent the company's shares soaring during 1720, only for the price to spectacularly crash. Henrietta's future father-in-law fled to the continent, but later returned after being pardoned.

Floral displays in the centre of Ullenhall, as seen outside the Old Post Office, now a private house, recall Lady Luxborough's gardening interest.

Field sports like hawking inspired Arden poet William Shenstone, a close friend of Lady Luxborough.

The Henley Road lodge at the entrance to Barrells Hall is now a very modern and luxurious house.

Her nine-year marriage ended when she separated from her husband amidst rumours of a "gallantry", possibly with John Dalton, the tutor of the son of Lady Hertford, future Duchess of Somerset, or with Warwickshire poet William Somerville.

Historians question whether either story is true, but it appears certain that Lady Luxborough either fled from some degree of domestic unhappiness, or was banished, to Ullenhall in 1736, and was not allowed access to her two children.

While she never divorced, she did not see her husband again. He became Lord Luxborough in 1746 and then Earl of Catherlough in 1763, seven years after Henrietta died.

At Barrells Hall, Henrietta turned to gardening and literature, and encouraged local minor poets including Somerville to visit her. Soon, others of like mind followed.

Somerville, the eldest son of a country gentleman and devotee of hunting, was born at Edstone near Woottton Wawen in 1675, and was educated at Winchester College and New College, Oxford. His best-known work was *The Chase*, while he also wrote *The Two Springs*, a fable, *Hobbinol, or the Rural Games*, describing the Cotswold Games, and *Field Sports*, a poem about hawking.

Then there was William Shenstone, a poet born in Halesowen, where he later inherited an estate. He was educated at Solihull School along with another future Arden literary figure and member of the Luxborough circle, Richard Jago.

Born in 1715, Jago was the son of the rector of Beaudesert, also Richard Jago, and himself became a minister, both curate and rector at Snitterfield. His best-known work was *The Blackbirds*, published under another name in 1753.

At Pembroke College, Oxford, Shenstone met yet another of the future Barrells Hall group, Richard Graves, author of *The Spiritual Quixote*, published in 1773. Graves became rector of Claverton near Bath.

Lady Luxborough wrote many letters to Shenstone over 16 years from 1739. He saved them, describing them as having been "written with abundant ease, politeness, and vivacity; in which she was scarce equalled by any woman of her time." They were published in 1775. Did Henrietta have closer feelings for Shenstone?

Horace Walpole, the eighteenth-century politician and writer, described Lady Luxborough, as "lusty" with "a great black bush of hair."

Her activities and the number of male visitors led to wild gossip and speculation in Ullenhall, which has never forgotten her.

Her body was interred at Wootton Wawen, and later moved to a mausoleum built in the grounds of Barrells Hall. Dismantled in 1830, a family vault was built at the village chapel to replace it.

Lady Luxborough's ghost is said to haunt the ruins of the hall, which was badly damaged by fire in 1933.

Her husband, whose second wife was childless, hypocritically enjoyed a relationship with Jane Davies of Moat House Farm in Ullenhall.

Jane moved to London, bore him four children, changed her name by deed poll to Knight and thereby reinforced his family's connection with the Ullenhall area.

Ullenhall's delightful village pub was known as the Catherlough Arms in the eighteenth century, in honour of the family. It later became the Winged Spur, its current name, taken from the Knight family emblem.

The name Ullenhall means 'Olafs Hall', the home of a Saxon settler.

The village developed in the thirteenth century around the then-new church of St Mark, now known as the 'old chapel.'

After it was decimated by bubonic plaque, the village moved to its present site.

The present church of St Mary was built in 1875 by the Newton family, who bought Barrells Hall in 1856.

Ullenhall, like so many English villages, once boasted several traditional shops and businesses, including a bakery, a blacksmith, a garage and general stores. Unable to compete with bigger businesses elsewhere, they have long since been converted into houses.

While Ullenhall remains very much a traditional village, nearby Oldberrow to the south is part of a sprawling sparsely-populated parish which also includes the scattered settlements of Morton Bagot and Spernal.

The Old Bakery in Ullenhall.

Lonely Oldberrow church with its half-timbered tower.

The tiny Holy Trinity church of Morton Bagot.

Oldberrow's lonely church of St Mary has features which date from the twelfth century, but was mostly rebuilt in 1875.

In 1253 Henry III granted Adam Dispenser permission to hold a weekly market on Wednesdays at Oldberrow, and a fair on the eve, feast, and morrow of St John the Evangelist, but it is difficult to see today that this all-but-deserted place had any importance other than agriculture.

There is no village of Morton Bagot as such, but a series of farms and cottages. Its second name is taken from William Bagot who held the manor of Morton in the time of Edward I, and whose family sold it to Roger de Conyngesby in 1296.

Morton Bagot's diminutive parish church of Holy Trinity which stands on a mound next to a large half-timbered barn dates from the late thirteenth century. The south porch and the tiled roofs and bell-turret were added around Shakespeare's time.

Now to the villages to the east of Henley.

Take the A4189 from the crossroads at the southern end of the town, and you will soon arrive at the little waterside gem that is Preston Bagot.

One of the finest views to be had anywhere in Arden is that from the hill on which this hamlet's little eleventh-century church of All Saints with its two Norman semi-circular arched doorways stands.

You can look out to neighbouring Beaudesert and Henley – which were both once part of Preston, the "parish of the priests" – and southwards towards the Cotswolds.

Preston after the Norman Conquest was far more important than it is today, but it was the influence of the newer church built next to the castle at Beaudesert that brought about its sharp decline in fortune.

William de Newburgh, Earl of Warwick, gave the manor of Preston to Ingeram Bagot, hence its second name. In 1235, it was held by Simon Bagoth.

Preston Bagot still has its half-timbered manor house, facing on to the main road, although it is a private residence not open to the public.

Preston's church was saved in 1878 by the architect J.A. Chatwin who in effect recreated a 'medieval' church by raising the height and adding a Romanesque chancel arch. The window was designed so that at sunset, the dying sun strikes the altar cross.

When the little church was investigated for damp, two skeletons were found between the inner and outer walls, and were given a decent Christian burial.

A surviving pocket of woodland at Morton Bagot.

Above:
A coal wharf was once sited here on the canal at Preston Bagot.

Right:
Preston Bagot's half-timbered manor with its herringbone brick infilling.

Preston Bagot's hilltop church of All Saints.

Preston Bagot churchyard contains the grave of a John Shakespeare, who died aged 80 in 1840. It is not known if he was related to the Bard.

Lost in the woods at the top of Yarningale Common.

The old Baptist chapel at Yarningale, which dates from 1881, has long since closed.

Dividing the scattering of houses that comprises Preston is the Stratford-upon-Avon Canal, which passes beneath the A4189 from Henley to Claverdon and Warwick.

Today, the most frequented building in Preston Bagot is the Crabmill public house, which dates back three centuries. The name refers to crab apples used to make cider.

Before Claverdon is reached, Ossetts Hole Lane turns off to Yarningale Common.

I have always loved this place, ever since my parents brought me here in dad's Triumph Standard 10 for afternoon ramblings.

It has always had a true 'dingly dell' feel, with farmsteads, houses and a very isolated Baptist chapel, scattered around what was/is historically public grazing land, and a wooded hill girdled by thick briars which always yielded an endless supply of sumptuous blackberries.

There was always something magical about Yarningale, which offered a unique sense of spaciousness, freedom and intrigue. A maze of paths led from the common into the wood, amd if you came back two seasons later and tried to retrace your steps, you would never find the same route again, no matter how hard you tried.

Yarningale has always been a popular spot for picnics. As a nine year old, I fondly recall that an ice cream van was sometimes parked there, and mom once returned from it with a sixpenny kit to make a balsa wood glider for me to play with on the common. Those golden times before computer games!

Today, I like to think of it as an unsullied piece of the old forest. Yes, the old homesteads are now the very desirable residences of millionaires, but it still remains unspoiled. Maybe this is how ancient Arden appeared when the first clearings appeared, and perhaps the wood at the top has been there from the days when all you would see from the top of the hill would have been a canopy of green stretching to the horizon. It is hard not to imagine this as quintessential Arden of old.

Further to the east is Claverdon, where the Spencers were lords of the manor. They are the same Spencers who have their seat at Althorp in Northamptonshire, and who included Diana, Princess of Wales, among them, although she was not a direct descendant of the Claverdon line.

In the fifteenth-century church of St Michaels and All Angels, a magnificent alabaster tomb and monument to Thomas Spencer can be seen. He was the second son of Sir John Spencer of Althorp, who died aged 82 in 1629.

Thomas himself had the monument erected, as he had no immediate family. He may also have built the great Stone Manor, an eccentric three-story building which puzzles historians. Some think it was built as a defensive tower house, a rare occurrence in the Midlands.

On the other side of the chancel from the Spencer memorial is one to Sir Francis Galton FRS, who founded the 'science' of eugenics.

A half-cousin of Charles Darwin, Galton became influenced by his groundbreaking work *On The Origin Of Species*.

In 1869, Galton published his own book, *Hereditary Genius*, claiming that 'good' families were more likely to produce intelligent and talented children, and therefore it was possible to produce a highly-gifted race of men through arranged marriages.

On the other hand, you could reach a similar goal by "discouraging" inferior people to breed at all, he argued.

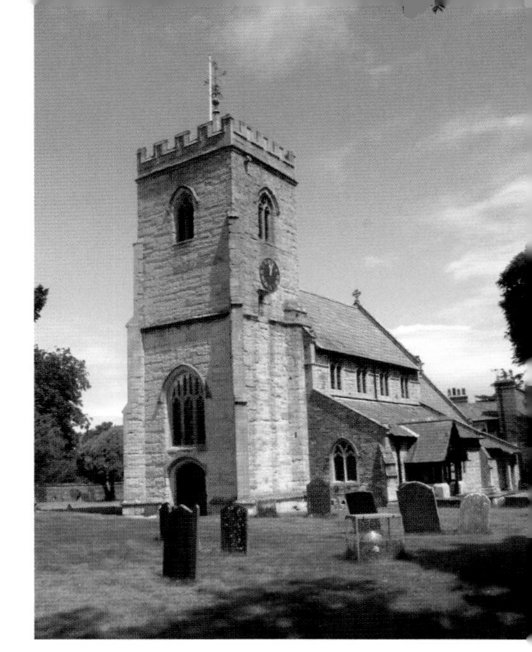

Claverdon's church of St Michael and All Angels dates from the fifteenth century.

The Crown Inn at Claverdon.

The Spencer memorial in Claverdon church.

These ideas formed the backbone of the American Eugenics Society founded in 1926 . . . and were later adopted by Hitler and his henchmen.

US supporters of eugenics successfully campaigned for the sterilisation of retarded and epileptic people in more than half the states. Only when the excesses of Nazi Germany became known was eugenics discredited, but few would directly blame Galton for the death camps.

On two far more positive notes, Galton also developed identification by fingerprints, and his work *Meteorgraphica,* published in 1863, formed the basis of modern weather charts.

The name Claverdon comes from the early English 'claefer dun' which means 'clover hill': indeed, there is still much clover around its leafy lanes.

Its most photographed building is the seventeenth-century roadside forge with its horseshoe-based archway, and which has been converted into an office.

Turning north through winding country lanes leads to the pretty canalside village of Lowsonford, with its Fleur-de-Lys public house, famous for its meat pies. Every two years a flower show is run jointly with the neighbouring village of Rowington.

The seventeenth-century forge on the main road is Claverdon's trademark feature.

Lowsonford's Fleur de Lys public house, famous for its meat pies.

A summer's day on the Stratford-upon-Avon Canal, as seen from the gardens of the Fleur de Lys.

4

THE CELTIC RIVER MEETS A ROMAN TOWN

Wootton Wawen, Aston Cantlow, Great Alne, Alcester

At Henley, the Alne is swelled by Hunger Hill Brook from Ullenhall, which conservationists prize for its crayfish, a protected freshwater species of lobster.

Beyond Blackford Mill, the river heads south into open pastureland for a mile, before being joined by its longest tributary the Tapster Brook, which drains the Tapster Valley, an unspoilt woodland backwater until the M40 between Solihull and London was built. The Tapster Brook also runs at the foot of the hill on which Baron Archer's Umberslade obelisk stands, therefore completing a sort of circle here.

At this junction comes the Alne's finest hour, when it fills a huge manmade lake in front of Wootton Hall, a fabulous Italianate mansion built in 1637. This pool, a spectacular and harmonic combination of the natural and artificial, was created by building two weirs across the river to the west of the main road to Stratford at Wootton Wawen.

Now converted into flats, the hall was historically home to various Catholic families, mainly the Caringtons, and also Lady Fitzherbert, who secretly married the Prince Regent, the future George IV, in 1785. Her ghost is one of several reported in the hall; another is that of Sir Charles Smith, murdered by his valet in France in 1664. His heart was brought home to the hall in a wooden box which was rediscovered there in late Victorian times.

In 1860, servant Betty Harris saw a man's figure in the old dairy courtyard. When the dairy was pulled down the following year, skeletons of a man and a woman were found.

Many old houses have romantic tales of secret passageways, but here they are true, for a 300-yard tunnel runs from the house to a spot beneath the main A3400. It may have been an escape route for Catholic priests persecuted under the reign of the protestant Elizabeth I, and for who discovery meant death.

The name Wootton Wawen is Saxon for 'farm by a wood' owned by Wagen, also remembered by nearby Wawens Moor, and the last Saxon thane to rule the area before the Norman Conquest.

Opposite: The Alne cascades over the weirs at Wootton Hall.

Saxon heritage is the outstanding feature of the eighth-century parish church of St Peter, perched on a hill above the Alne, and which claims to be the oldest in Warwickshire.

The original settlers in the forest clearing here were ancient Britons, and the first church mentioned in a charter of the Saxon King Aethelbald may have been founded by one Aethelric for spreading the Christian faith to local pagans.

An early Anglo-Saxon network of local farms became a territory called Stoppingas, which also included the hamlets of Aspley, Botley, Edstone, Mockley and Ullenhall. Stoppingas in turn became part of the small kingdom of the Hwicce, and later Mercia.

The church was constructed from timber and thatch, but later rebuilt in stone. First dedicated to St Mary, it changed to St Peter a century after the conquest.

It then came under the jurisdiction of French Benedictine friars who built a priory on the church field. Friars persuaded locals to join the Crusades to the Holy Land.

Henry VI closed the priory in 1443, during the Hundred Years War with France, when French monks were out of favour.

St Peter's parish church dates from the 700s.

Above:
Inside the church of St Peter is the tomb of Francis Smith, lord of Wootton manor, a contemporary of Shakespeare who died in 1604.

The church was later given to Henry's new King's College in Cambridge, which is still patron of the parish.

Today the church is marketed as the Saxon Sanctuary, a tourist attraction.

Legend has it that Shakespeare was a friend of the vicar and frequented Wootton Wawen while courting Anne Hathaway. He would therefore have known Wootton's Bull's Head, which dates from 1317.

The next village downstream is the quaint-sounding Aston Cantlow. 'Aston' is Saxon for 'eastern farmstead' while 'Cantlow' refers to the Norman John de Cantelope, who held the manor in 1205.

A descendant of his became a saint, one of only two in Britain celebrated in the village where they lived.

Thomas de Cantelupe, Chancellor to Henry III, and also Bishop of Hereford, was also the last Englishman to be made a saint before Henry VIII halted beatification.

Born in 1218 at Hambleden in Buckinghamshire, Thomas taught canon law at Oxford University and became its chancellor in 1262.

However, he sided with rebel Simon de Montfort during the Baron's War. After de Montfort was killed at Evesham, Thomas fled into exile, but returned and became a key adviser to Edward I. Later falling out with the Archbishop of Canterbury, Thomas was excommunicated in 1282, the year when he died in Italy.

The Cantelupes had a moated castle filled with Alne water, but only traces survive.

The village is better remembered for the wedding of William Shakespeare's parents in 1557.

In those days, Aston Cantlow was a thriving trading centre alongside the Alne and its watermills, and sufficiently prosperous to have its own Guild House, which dates from the sixteenth century and stands opposite the beautiful church of St John the Baptist.

Did the newlyweds celebrate in the splendid half-timbered King's Head next door?

The river next encounters 'twin' villages dedicated to it, the tiny cluster of houses that is Little Alne, and the far bigger Great Alne.

Top: *The Bull's Head pub in Wootton Wawen, which dates back to 1317.*

Middle: *Aston Cantlow's sixteenth-century Guild House.*

Bottom: *The King's Head in Aston Cantlow, another of the classic inns of old Arden.*

Thatched cottage and garden in Great Alne.

Great Alne was originally called Ruwenalne or Round Alne, the 'round' meaning 'rough'.

Its manor dated from AD809 and belonged to the Abbey of Winchcombe until Henry VIII dissolved the monasteries, after which it was sold off.

In 1876, Great Alne Hall was built on the site of the manor house. Replaced by a more modest version in the 1930s, the site was later covered by an engineering works and light industrial units.

In 1942, the Rockwell Standard plant was set up in Great Alne as a shadow factory for bombed production lines in Coventry. Its production of machinery for the war effort brought hordes of workers into the village . . . along with a few German incendiary bombs. The name of the village pub, the Mother Huff Cap, is unique, and derives from a local verse:

'Twixt Michaelmas and Martinmas
Old dame began to brew,
With half a pint of old malt
And half a pint of new.
First twenty gallons of Huff my Cap,
Then twenty gallons worse than that,
Then twenty gallons as amber clear,
And then she brewed the servants' beer.

The Mother Huff Cap: a pub name unique in Britain.

Great Alne is linked with neighbouring Kinwarton, as the village churches have always been under one rector.

Tiny Kinwarton's special feature is its medieval dovecote which housed birds to supply the table of the lord of the manor and which is now looked after by the National Trust.

Beyond here, the Alne lends its name again, this time to the once-walled Roman fortress town of Alcester.

Settled before the coming of the Romans, Alcester occupies the south-western corner of Arden, where the ancient Saltway from Droitwich to Stratford-upon-Avon meets the Roman road Ryknield or Icknield Street.

An important market town throughout history, Alcester had a thriving twelfth-century Benedictine monastery later given to the Greville family by Henry VIII at the dissolution.

For those who wish to visit a town well endowed with half-timbered buildings, Alcester presents a quieter and less commercialised alternative to Stratford. Centuries-old Malt Mill Lane and Butter Street are outstanding examples of Tudor steets.

Great Alne was served by a six-mile railway, running between the Great Western Railway's Stratford-upon-Avon line at Bearley, and Alcester, where it joined the Midland Railway's Birmingham-Evesham route, between 1876 and 1917, when it was ripped up for the war effort, and between 1922 and 1951, after it was relaid. After closure, Great Alne station became its post office and later a private house.

The Alne on its last lap through Arden heading towards Kinwarton.

Butter Street was so called because it sold perishables; the overhanging buildings and cramped street served to keep it in the shade for most of the day, allowing produce to remain fresh.

The parish church of St Nicholas houses the tomb of Fulke Greville, grandfather of Fulke Greville, the 1st Baron Brooke, (1554–1628), who was born at nearby Beauchamp Court and served as Chancellor of the Exchequer. In 1621 he was made a peer and was granted Warwick Castle.

Baron Brooke was also an accomplished poet and dramatist, best remembered for his autobiography of Sir Philip Sidney.

Buried in St Mary's church in Warwick, the baron died after being stabbed by a servant who felt cheated in his master's will, and who then turned the blade on himself.

Today Alcester is a major point on the 100 mile-long Heart of England Way long-distance walking route, and also has Roman Alcester, a free museum devoted to local artefacts from the first to fourth centuries.

The superbly-preserved medieval dovecote at Kinwarton.

Leaning half-timbered buildings in Alcester's Malt Mill Lane are a Tudor timewarp.

In early June, Alcester holds its Court Leet charity street market, its medieval leet dating from 1299 having much the same origins, purpose and officials as that of Henley further upstream. On the first Monday and Tuesday of October, the town holds its annual mop fair, with amusement rides.

At Oversley Bridge, to the south of the town, the Alne flows into the Arrow, a river which runs down part of the western edge of Arden, through Studley and Coughton, and which a short distance later meets the Avon. It may well be a meeting too soon, for after prolonged rainfall their channels struggle to cope, and the town suffered serious floods in 1956, 1998 and 2007.

Alcester's Butter Street, where shade was a big asset.

The clock on Alcester's St Nicholas' church is fixed in an unusual position on the south-west corner of the fourteenth-century tower, so it can be seen from High Street.

Baron Brooke, a friend of the playwright Ben Jonson and poet Edmund Spenser, built Alcester Market Hall.

Classic Tudor buildings in Alcester's High Steeet.

Made from mighty Arden oaks: houses in Alcester's Meeting Lane.

The watermeadows of the River Arrow, which later absorbs the Alne, below the parish church of St Mary, Studley, where watermills made the village a major centre of needlemaking.

5

GUNPOWDER, TREASON AND PLOT

Baddesley Clinton, Coughton Court

At Hindlip Hall near Worcester, the headquarters of West Mercia Police since 1967, the occupants should know more about arrests than anyone else.

For the Georgian manor house stands on the site of the earlier Hindlip House, in which, four centuries ago, three arrests marked one of the most notorious episodes of terrorism in British history, and some of the darkest days of old Arden.

The Gunpowder Plot

Two of the key plotters, Catholic priests Father Henry Garnet, the leading Jesuit in England, who had just fled hotfoot from the forest, and Father Edward Oldcorne, along with lay brother Ralph Ashley, were literally holed up in the hall for 11 days while the agents of the Crown sought with a vengeance all those involved in the scheme to blow up the Houses of Parliament with James I inside.

The Jesuit pair hid in 'priest holes' inside the house. These purpose-built secret compartments were a feature of many houses where the Catholic aristocracy who had refused to convert to the Protestantism of Elizabeth I hid priests who privately ministered to them.

Hindlip's 11 priest holes were the work of builder Nicholas Owen, and commissioned by Thomas Habington, who inherited the estate from his father John, an official at Elizabeth's court in 1582.

Thomas had already been in trouble for his militant Catholicism; he and his elder brother Edward had been involved in the Babington Plot to overthrow Elizabeth and place her cousin Mary Queen of Scots on the throne.

Edward was beheaded, but Thomas, a godson of Elizabeth, was pardoned after a spell in the Tower of London.

Opposite: *Coughton Court, where the Gunpowder Plotters waited for news.*

A contemporary sketch of the Gunpowder Plot conspirators by Dutch artist Crispijn van de Passe the Elder.

Owen also hid at Hindlip alongside the priests, and was the first to come out, their pursuers having sat it out in the parlour until their quarry could no longer bear conditions so cramped that they could not even straighten their legs.

The captured plotters would soon meet the vilest of fates.

Nearby Arden had for decades been a festering hotbed of Catholicism, a welcome bolthole not only to those who refused to give up the old ways and chose to worship in private, but for the Catholic 'fundamentalists' who sought to bring about swift change.

The great divide between the two faiths dated back to Henry VIII's break with Rome.

However, it was the reign of Henry's Catholic zealot daughter, Queen Mary which polarised public support for Protestantism.

The public burnings of 'heretics' along with many other cruelties left Mary so hated that the day of her death was nationally celebrated by bonfires for 200 years afterwards.

Catholics became a minority under Mary's half-sister Elizabeth, but included many rich and powerful families who were willing to merely bide their time.

After Elizabeth died in 1603, her cousin, James VI of Scotland, son of Mary Queen of Scots, ascended the English throne. Catholics who hoped he would favour their cause were soon bitterly disappointed to find he had no intention of doing so.

Thirteen angry young Catholics decided to take matters into their own hands, and in what might now be viewed as an early seventeenth-century version of 9/11, planned to blow up Parliament along with most of the country's nobles, bishops and MPs.

Catholic soldier and munitions expert Guy, or Guido, Fawkes hid 36 barrels of gunpowder under the House of Lords, aiming to light the fuse during the state opening of Parliament on 5 November 1605.

Much of the plot originated in Arden. Ringleader Robert Catesby may have been born at Lapworth, where he later owned property, or possibly in Northamptonshire, to a wealthy Catholic family in 1605.

Baddesley Clinton, a moated manor near Lapworth, then owned by Henry Ferrers, was a Catholic safe house which concealed Jesuit priests, who faced death if discovered, and three priest holes like those in Hindlip House survive today.

The holes proved their worth on at least one occasion, in 1591 when a conference of Jesuit priests was raided by local authorities to no avail.

The Catholic Vaux sisters, who rented the house from Henry Ferrers, had secretly sheltered Father Garnet. It was Anne Vaux who ordered the priest holes to be built by our friend Owen.

Father John Gerard, author of *Autobiography of an Elizabethan*, and several other priests and lay assistants awoke to find the house surrounded.

The stable boys armed themselves with farm implements to prevent the authorities from gaining entry, claiming the lady of the house had not yet risen, and buying time for the priests to be hidden.

For four hours, Father Gerard and his colleagues stood ankle deep in the freezing waters of the moat as the house was searched.

A hand-coloured postcard of Baddesley Clinton, one of the real jewels of the Forest of Arden.

Baddesley Clinton is the finest of all the surviving medieval moated manors of old Arden.

Nothing was found, and the hunters left after Anne Vaux paid them off with 12 gold pieces.

Religion and rebellion apart, Baddesley Clinton is one of the most important historic houses of Arden.

The northern part of Arden is liberally littered with the remains of medieval moated manors, as the great clay bed which lies below much of the forest is superb for water retention. While moats were first designed for defensive purposes, they also supplied fish and fowl for the dining table.

Most of the moated houses disappeared centuries ago, but by far the best surviving example is Baddesley Clinton.

A Grade I listed building and scheduled ancient monument dating back to the fourteenth century, it was bought by John Brome, Under Treasurer of England in 1438.

His son Nicholas rebuilt the adjacent parish church of St Michael as penance for no less a misdeed than killing the parish priest.

When Nicholas Brome died in 1517, the house passed to his daughter, who married the High Sheriff of Warwickshire, Sir Edward Ferrers.

Henry Ferrers (1549–1633), an avid collector of historical data and nicknamed 'The Antiquary', made many improvements to Baddesley Clinton. He began the tradition of stained glass windows representing the family's coat of arms and may also have built the Great Hall.

The sylvan walk from Baddesley Clinton manor house to the church of St Michael.

The church of St Michael is also known as the 'Church of the Expiation' because it was improved by Nicholas Brome as penance for killing its minister, after he returned to Baddesley Clinton to find him being over-familiar with his wife in the parlour. Both the king and the Pope pardoned Nicholas for the killing, said to have taken place in the Library Room, which some say is haunted.

The Forestry Commission's Hay Wood near Baddesley Clinton is open to the public as a nature reserve.

The house was bought in 1980 by the National Trust from Thomas Walker, a relative of the Ferrers who later adopted their name.

But back to the plot. One of the leading conspirators, Sir Everard Digby, rented Coughton Court near Alcester from the Throckmortons, a leading Catholic family of the forest.

Furthermore, chief conspirator Robert Catesby's mother was a Throckmorton, as was fellow conspirator Francis Tresham. The Coughton estate, incidentally, had been in the Throckmorton family since 1409.

The conspirators leased a building belonging to none other than Henry Ferrers near the Houses of Parliament, and began digging a tunnel from it.

Digby and a group of supporters waited with bated breaths at Coughton to hear whether their plan had succeeded.

To their horror, Catesby's servant Thomas Bates arrived hotfoot on 6 November with news that Fawkes had been caught red handed, holding the fuses, and that the conspirators were unmasked.

Present were Father Garnet, who had celebrated mass for the Feast of All Saints in the house a few days before, Father Oswald Tesimond, the confessor to Robert Catesby, Digby's family, Owen and the Vaux sisters who were related to the Throckmortons.

The plotters fled first to Dunchurch near Rugby, where other supporters had been waiting for news at the Red Lion Inn (now a private residence called Guy Fawkes House) and then to Holbeach House near Kingswinford in Staffordshire.

Under the leadership of Sir Richard Walsh, the sheriffs of Warwickshire and Worcestershire stormed that house on 8 November, killing several plotters.

Gunpowder failed the conspirators for the second time in three days: their supply had become wet during their flight from Coughton, and when they dried it out in front of a fire at the house, it blew up.

Walsh's crack marksman John Streete felled Catesby and another plotter, Thomas Percy, with a single shot.

The others, including Digby, were arrested and imprisoned at Worcester before being transported to London to await their show trial, their fates a foregone conclusion.

On 27 January 1606, Fawkes and those conspirators still alive were found guilty of high treason and sentenced to death.

Three days later, Digby and three others were dragged through the streets before being hanged, drawn and quartered in front of the crowds in St Paul's courtyard.

It was the turn of Guy Fawkes and others the next day, but he cheated the worst of the barbarities by jumping from the gallows ladder and breaking his neck.

Owen died under torture in the Tower of London, while the other three caught at Hindlip Hall were hung, drawn and quartered.

Coughton Court, which lies on the westernmost edge of Arden, the house with its magnificent façade directly facing the Roman road Ryknield or Icknield Street which is now the A435, still remains a Throckmorton stronghold.

The house, the oldest part being the gatehouse which dates from 1530, has been owned by the National Trust since 1946. The Throckmorton family now holds a 300-year lease and manages the estate for the trust.

Set in extensive grounds including a formal garden, a river and a lake, the house is open to the public and has an exhibition about the plot. Heraldic glass windows in the Drawing Room, reopened in 1956 after being blocked up for 130 years commemorate the marriages of the Throckmortons to the leading Catholic families, including the Catesbys and Treshams.

The mothers of Catesby and Tresham were the sisters Anne and Muriel Throckmorton, granddaughters of the original builder, Sir George Throckmorton, and sisters as well of the lord of the manor in 1605, Thomas Throckmorton. Two other conspirators, Robert and Thomas Wintour, were also great-grandchilden of Sir George Throckmorton.

Father Tesimond escaped to flee to the continent, but the women who had been waiting at Coughton with him were let off with mere questioning,

Catesby's father, however, spent much of his life imprisoned for offences related to his Catholicism.

And as for Henry Ferrers of Baddesley Clinton, unlike Fawkes and his associates, he was never convicted of any offence.

Autumnal perfection in the grounds of Coughton Court.

Sunset over Engine House Pool at Earlswood Lakes.

6

THE SPARKLING RIVER OF SOLIHULL

Earlswood, Cheswick Green, Shirley, Solihull, Barston, Hampton-in-Arden, Packington and Maxstoke

The Blythe, a meandering silver stream which runs for just 28 miles from start to finish, is the principal river of northern Arden.

With its luscious green water meadows, centuries-old fords and classic stone bridges, it is one of the great prizes of the old forest, having escaped the excesses of the modern world that is now on its doorstep.

Renowned for the richness of its wildlife, the Blythe is a designated Site of Special Scientific interest as it is considered a prime example of a lowland river on clay.

Its journey begins in roadside ditches at Portway near Wythall, which link to form Spring Brook, as the first four miles of the Blythe are known.

Crossing nearby Ladbrook Golf Course, the stream arrives at the 13th tee . . . and the splendidly-preserved wooded site of a medieval moated manor house, the first of many in the Blythe valley. This was the hunting lodge of the earls of Warwick for 400 years.

Legends say it was the birthplace of Guy of Warwick, son of a steward to a Saxon earl of Warwick who had to fight the Saracens in the Holy Land, kill a dragon, a wild boar and a Danish giant to win the hand of his master's daughter.

Spring Brook fills Arden's own 'inland sea', Earlswood Lakes.

This network of three reservoirs. Engine House Pool, Windmill Pool and Terry's Pool, the first two divided by a causeway carrying a public road, contains 34 million cubic feet of water for topping up the Stratford-upon-Avon Canal.

It became a hugely-popular daytrip destination for Birmingham families from Victorian times onwards, and was known as the "Scarborough of the Midlands."

The stream which flows from the great earthen dam is known for the first time as the Blythe.

A heatwave at Earlswood Lakes in 1955.

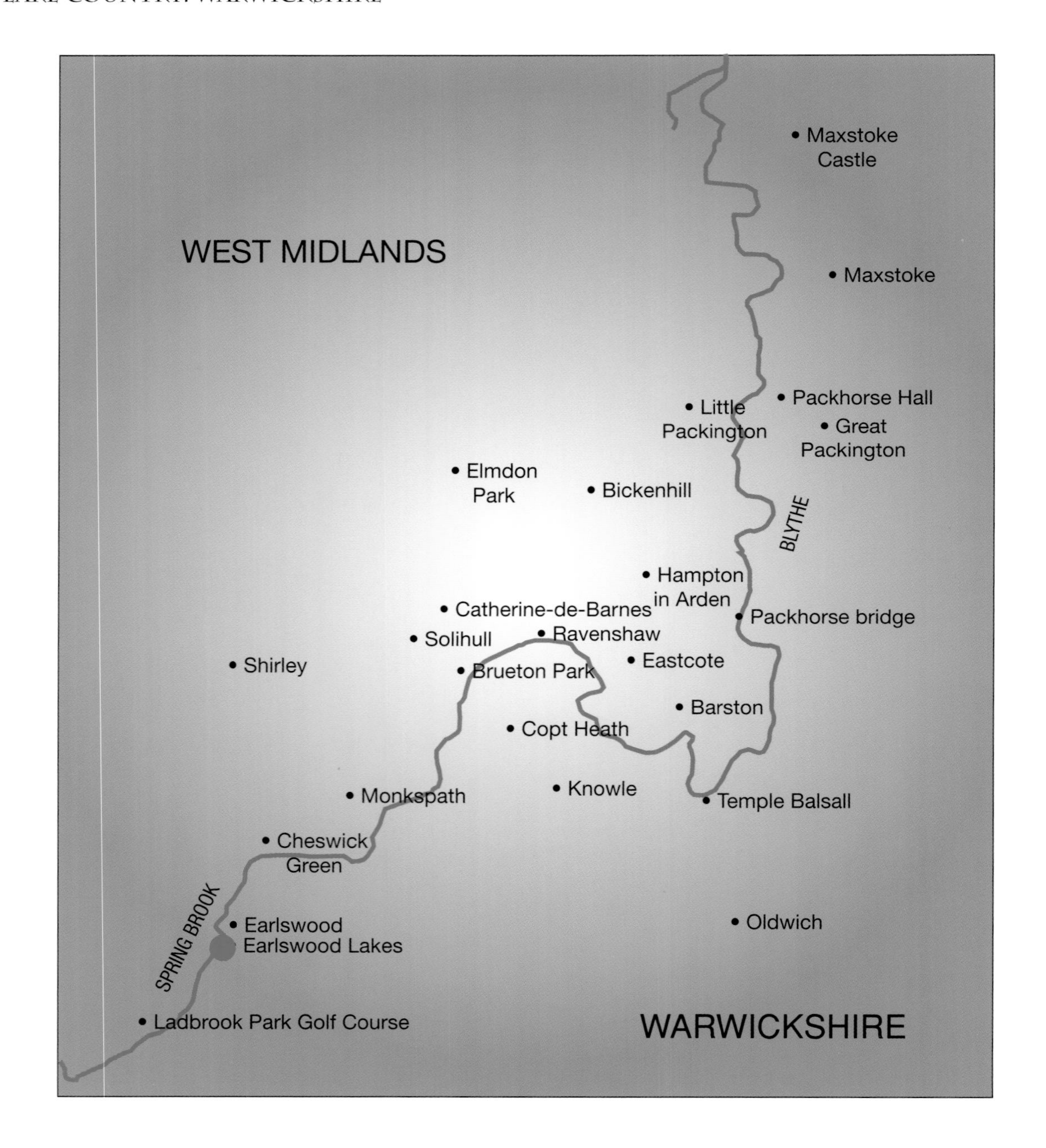
Maxstoke Castle
WEST MIDLANDS
Maxstoke
Little Packington
Packhorse Hall
Great Packington
Elmdon Park
Bickenhill
BLYTHE
Hampton in Arden
Catherine-de-Barnes
Packhorse bridge
Solihull
Ravenshaw
Shirley
Brueton Park
Eastcote
Barston
Copt Heath
Monkspath
Knowle
Temple Balsall
Cheswick Green
SPRING BROOK
Earlswood
Earlswood Lakes
Oldwich
Ladbrook Park Golf Course
WARWICKSHIRE

Feeding time at Earlswood Lakes.

The old steam pumping house which lifted water from the lakes into the canal.

As payment for the land taken for the reservoirs, the canal company paid Tanworth-in-Arden's churchwardens £969 8s 9d.

The money was used to build a new church alongside the canal at Salter Street, unusually dedicated to the Irish Roman Catholic St Patrick. Completed in 1840, the striking Gothic tower was added in 1899.

The name Earlswood signifies that the area was owned by the Earl of Warwick.

Cheswick Green dates back to the twelfth century and means "cheese farm". It served a colossal moated homestead, the Mount, home of Roger de Ulehale, who was granted the manor of Monkspath by the Earl of Warwick by 1184.

The site was developed as pleasure gardens with weekend tea dances during Edwardian times, but the venture failed. After the First World War, the Mount estate was split into tiny plots and sold to Birmingham families for weekend homes, but many of them stayed permanently, and a shanty town of wooden dwellings mushroomed.

The inhabitants sold out to a housebuilder in the sixties, and a suburban 'village of the seventies' sprang up. Sadly, the developer infilled the moat and bulldozed part of the Mount despite protests, before going bust.

The river passes Shirley Golf Course, which replaced a racecourse that operated from the mid-nineteenth century until 1953.

The name Blythe was first recorded in the time of Henry II and comes from the Old English 'blitha' which means "calm and flowing" – yet as with the Alne, heavy cloudbursts, prolonged rainfall or snow meltwaters quickly transform it into a raging torrent, with the clay beds preventing surplus water seeping away.

Monkspath Bridge was built in 1339 to take the Kings Highway from Solihull to Henley-in-Arden safely across the Blythe.

Earlswood Lakes in deep midwinter.

An early twentieth-century view of Solihull's Hillfield Hall, part of which is now the Stables pub.

Now it carries the A34, which leads northwards into Shirley, a settlement recorded in 1240 as a 'bright clearing' in the forest. Rapid twentieth-century suburban expansion has left Shirley as a mile of shops and countless housing estates.

Near the river lay the medieval hamlet of Shelly, now swamped by the modern Monkspath and Hillfield housing estates, but half-timbered Shelly Farm survives as a pub.

Beyond Blythe Bridge which takes Widney Manor Road over an ancient ford, the river flows through fields which were part of the Longdon Hall estate owned by Annabella Milbanke Noel, wife of the Romantic poet Lord Byron.

The womanising Byron was already causing a public scandal by his relationship with his half-sister Augusta when he married Annabella, daughter of Lady Melbourne, in 1815.

The marriage lasted only a year before Annabella returned to her parents.

Byron left England and died of a fever in Greece in 1824 at the age of 36, but his wife lived until 1860, founding an agricultural boarding school at Copt Heath Farm. Her name and that of her grandson, Earl Lovelace, are remembered by local roads.

The next river crossing is Sandals Bridge, which carried the old Warwick Road, now replaced by a bypass. Here, the Blythe was dammed to create a millpond for fifteenth-century Sandwell Mill. The pool is now Brueton Park's lake and home to swans, ducks and Canada geese.

The artist John Constable visited nearby Malvern Hall and in 1809 painted the Blythe near Sandals Bridge.

After 200-years-old Monkspath Hall, a farm in Stratford Road, Monkspath, was bulldozed in December 1980, it transpired that the demolition contractor had been sent by owner Solihull Council to knock down only the outbuildings! After the incident made international headlines, it was rebuilt following an insurance claim and is now a private dwelling.

Grade II listed Shelly Farm is now a public house.

Wildlife at Brueton Park lake.

Solihull's parish church of St Alphege.

Brueton Park joins with adjacent Malvern Park, providing a green swathe of public open space leading into Solihull town centre.

Solihull, renowned as one of the most affluent towns in Britain today, was first recorded in 1170 as 'miry hill' (soily hill). Sitting atop a hill of red clay, dominated by the parish church of St Alphege, it was artificially created as a medieval 'newtown' by the de Limisi family, lords of the man of Ulverlei, to capitalise on the meeting of the trade routes from Birmingham to Warwick and Droitwich (the great salt-producing centre) to Coventry.

It replaced Olton, which became the 'old town' and diminished in importance after the twelfth century. The de Limisis lived at the great moated manor of Hobs Moat in the district of Solihull which now bears that name, and the earthwork survives.

St Alphege, or St Aelfheah, was born in AD953 to a noble family in the village of Weston near Bath and became prior of Glastonbury Abbey and abbot of Bath.

King Ethelred the Unready despatched Aelfheah to convert Viking invader Olaf Tryggyeson, King of Norway to Christianity. He succeeded, being made Archbishop of Canterbury in 1005 as a reward, but two years later, the Vikings seized Canterbury and took Aelfheah prisoner. He was killed by his jailers.

Today's modern cosmopolitan shopping centre is barely recognizable from the Solihull of half a century ago. Where today's big stores stand, there were narrow streets barely changed since medieval times including many half-timbered buildings, cottages, terraced dwellings and allotment patches. The town centre underwent major redevelopments in the sixties and nineties, the last producing the Touchwood Court shopping complex.

Stained glass window recording the martyrdom of St Alphege.

From Sandals Bridge, the Blythe flows to the ancient hamlet and ford of Ravenshaw, before twisting towards Eastcote, Barston and Temple Balsall, to be discussed in the next chapter. Barston was recorded in the Domesday Book as Bercestone, and Roman pottery has been found near Eastcote.

Turning back north, the Blythe reaches Hampton-in Arden, said to be Shakespeare's inspiration for *As You Like It*.

Hampton's name comes from the Saxon 'Hantone, the 'high village on the hill,' in this case the high land between the Blythe and its tributary the Shadowbrook.

In the twelfth century, Hampton was owned by the de Arden family, whose manor house stood next to the church, founded by Geoffrey de Wirce around 1130 on the site of the Saxon original. The spire was blasted by a lightning bolt in 1643 and crashed to the ground.

Sir Hugh Arden obtained a royal charter for a weekly Tuesday market in 1251.

Sir Frederick Peel MP, son of Sir Robert Peel, the founder of the police force, lived in Hampton. His illustrious father built the present manor house for him.

As Chief Railway Commissioner, Sir Frederick (1823–1906), persuaded trains to stop at little Hampton en route from London to Birmingham, placing it on the national map for the first time. After the railway arrived in 1840, Hampton had the 'in-Arden' tag added to differentiate it from other Hamptons.

This pleasant peaceful village might well have developed into a railway town the size of Crewe had a bizarre venture succeeded.

The Grand Union Canal at Solihull's outpost of Catherine-de-Barnes, named not after a woman but a man, Ketelberne, twelfth-century owner of the manor of Longdon.

Solihull's Elmdon Park offers sweeping views of the Birmingham skyline.

Elmdon is 'the hill of the elms', but this sweet chestnut, which could be 500 years old, steals the show in its park.

The tree-lined road through Copt Heath from Solihull to Knowle in Edwardian times.

The heart of Hampton-in-Arden a century ago.

The church of St Swithin in Barston.

Hampton's old railway station, now offices.

In 1836, at the height of the Railway Mania, the Birmingham & Derby Junction Railway was so determined to beat bitter rival the Midland Counties Railway to London that it bypassed Birmingham! A line closely following the Blythe was built from Whitacre to sleepy Hampton, linking there to the London to Birmingham railway.

For three years after the line opened in 1839, Hampton was one of the busiest railway junctions in Britain. However, the rivalries ended and the original route from Derby into Birmingham was completed. The Hampton line was then downgraded to a mere branch which saw little traffic and was ripped up in the early 1950s.

Yet this obscure railway can proudly claim to have been used by every monarch from Victoria onwards.

The Royal Train carried King George the Sixth and the future Elizabeth II on morale-boosting visits to West Midlands arms production factories during the Second World War. The train was stabled overnight in the deep cuttings of the line, safely out of sight of Nazi bombers.

The line's old Hampton station has been converted into offices.

One of Hampton's best-loved landmarks is the Packhorse Bridge which crosses the Blythe. It was built in the 1500s, possibly as part of the salt way from Droitwich.

From Stonebridge to the north east of Hampton, the Blythe winds through 300-acre Packington Park, famous for its trout fisheries and deer herds for over 250 years.

Charles I visited Packington before the Battle of Edgehill and his son, later Charles II, fled there after his defeat at Worcester, his escape was made possible by the gallantry of one Jane Lane, who carried the future king pillion on her horse.

The first Earl of Aylesford acquired Packington when he married Jane Lane's only daughter, and the present earl is his direct descendant.

Hampton-in-Arden parish church.

The hall was built in Oliver Cromwell's day while much of the grounds including the Hall Pool were designed by Capability Brown.

The composer Handel visited Packington as a guest of the fourth earl. In 1749, he designed the organ in St James' church, a red brick building with four domes in neo-classical style, built to celebrate the return to sanity of King George III.

The church is owned by the Aylesford family, but can be visited. The hall and park are not normally open to the public.

Across the Blythe lies the humbler Little Packington church of St Bartholomew with its unusual half-timbered spire, now converted into a private house.

One business you would not normally associate with a stately home is waste disposal, and here the Packington estate has remodelled the topography of Arden.

Instead of dumping rubbish into landfill sites, waste has been piled high to create a new hill on the flat landscape of the lower Blythe valley.

The sculpted hill looks every bit like the real thing, and forms a windbreak to shield Packington Hall from wintry blasts.

Hampton's famous Packhorse Bridge.

The Blythe then flows beneath the M6 to Maxstoke, where the village contains the ruins of a priory founded in 1331 by Admiral Sir William de Clinton, later Earl of Huntingdon.

A mile away lies the most magnificent of all the moated buildings in the Blythe valley. Private Maxstoke Castle was built by Sir William in 1345, but was designed more as a residence than as a military stronghold. Apart from the occasion when Cromwell's troops fired a cannon at it but missed, it has remained untouched by conflict.

It was there that Richard III spent the night before his death at the Battle of Bosworth on 22 August 1485: Henry VII came to Maxstoke to celebrate victory the next evening.

Inside the castle is the chair in which Henry was said to have been crowned on Bosworth Field.

The castle is opened to the public on a very limited number of days to raise money for charity.

Swarms of blue dragonflies still dart merrily over the surface of the Blythe on hot summer days while shoals of fish still appear plentiful. The water quality remains sparkling until the end, when this gleaming Arden river surrenders itself to the Tame, murky with the treated effluent from Birmingham's treatment works.

Hall Pool with Packington Hall to the right.

The gatehouse to the ruined Maxstoke Priory.

Sanity prevailed when St James' church at Packington was built.

Ancient Packington ford across the Blythe is deceptively deep.

Maxstoke Castle remains a private residence today at the end of this drive.

The true Mary Arden's House, Glebe Farm, which was painted by John Constable long before it was established as the real home of Shakespeare's mother.

7

THE SHAKESPEARES: SOLIHULL'S GREATEST FAMILY

Oldwich, Temple Balsall, Knowle, Packwood, Wroxall, Rowington, Snitterfield, Wilmcote

The story of the world's most influential writer of all time begins not in Stratford-upon-Avon, the mass haunt of international tourists, but in an obscure hamlet much nearer the other side of the great forest, in Solihull.

The history of William Shakespeare's ancestors remains vague, especially as the surname was fairly commonplace in the Midlands of the Middle Ages.

Shakespere, Shakspere, Shaksper, Shakkespere, Shakeshafte, Saxper, Shakstaff, Sakspere, Shagspere, and Chacsper – it is spelled in many different ways in records.

The name has a military background, meaning the wielding of a spear. One of the earliest records of the name is that of John Shakespeare at Freyndon, possibly Frittendon in Kent, in 1279. Five years later, a William Sakspere of Clopton in Gloucestershire was hanged for theft.

In 1487 Hugh Shakspere of Merton College, Oxford changed his surname to Sawndare because the surname had a 'vile reputation.' The first Warwickshire Shakespeare to be recorded was in 1358 when Thomas Shakespeare was arrested for murder in Coventry.

However, it is in today's metropolitan borough of Solihull, whose modern-day motto, *urbs in rure*, reflects its mixture of ancient Arden countryside and rapid suburban growth over the past century, that the ancestral roots of William Shakespeare's family lie.

A William Shakespeare was recorded in 1385 as serving on a coroner's jury in Balsall, a scattered settlement which now falls within Solihull. A Saxon name meaning 'Baeell's corner of land,' it is also the name of Balsall Common, a large commuter settlement midway between Solihull, Kenilworth and Coventry.

The rolling countryside around the hamlet of Oldwich, origin of the Shakespeare family, is typical of so much of Arden countryside today: the forest disappeared centuries ago, making way for settlements and agriculture, with the trees confined to hedgerows.

A surviving example of an ancient green lane near Oldwich. The muddy track, a right of way, is marked as an 'unclassified county road' by a signpost and is typical of many 'main' roads in the Arden of old.

The ceremonial robes of a Knight Templar.

The name Oldeditc, the ancient hamlet in Solihull where William Shakespeare's ancestors may have lived, survives today, as Oldwich.

Adam of Oldeditc (a tiny hamlet at Balsall whose name means 'lane with an old ditch' and is today spelled Oldwich) had a son believed to have given himself the surname Shakespeare. It is certainly possible that the Bard is descended from him.

Nearby tiny Temple Balsall, which lies on the Blythe, was one of many places in Britain owned by the Knights Templar, a monastic military order formed at the end of the eleventh century.

The Templars' original role was to protect Christian pilgrims journeying to the Holy Land. Warrior monks, a sort of English Taliban of the Middle Ages, took part in several Crusades, fighting alongside Richard the Lionheart.

Recognised by the Pope in 1113, the order took its name from its headquarters on the site of Jerusalem's Temple of Solomon, given to them by the city's king, Baldwin I.

Within two centuries, they became powerful enough to defy all authority save that of the Pope. Feared as warriors and respected for their charity, many envied them for their vast wealth and were suspicious of their secret ceremonies.

The capture of Jerusalem inspired great patriotic fervour amongst the English and around 1130, Templars from France were given land throughout England by King Stephen and his wife Matilda. Roger de Mowbray, son of a Norman knight favoured by Henry I, and who went on his first crusade in 1146, gave Balsall to the Templars.

In 1291, Acre, the last Christian stronghold in the Holy Land, fell to the Turks, leaving the Templars without a cause to fight.

The King of France, Philip the Fair, looked closely at their riches – and in 1308 had the Templars arrested on the trumped-up grounds of heresy, so he could seize their money and assets. Templars in England were also detained, including five at Balsall.

Everywhere, members of the order were tortured and dubious confessions extracted.

The Pope abolished the Templars in March 1312, transferring their properties to rival order the Knights Hospitallers, and on 19 March 1314, the last Grand Master of the Knights Templar, Jacques de Molay, was burned at the stake.

Around this time, the Keeper of the King's Wardrobe stripped the order's estate at Temple Balsall. Around 120 oak trees were felled, leaving only one on the manor, while 14 oxen, a cow, 40 bullocks and 40 pigs were driven to Windsor Park for consumption by the royal family.

Two of the stained glass windows inside St Mary's church at Temple Balsall reflect the building's history as one of the properties of the Knights Hospitallers.

Temple Balsall's unique church of St Mary built by the Knights Templar.

The great round stained glass window inside St Mary's church.

In 1322, Temple Balsall passed to the Hospitallers, forerunners of today's Order of St John, which maintains the St John Ambulance Brigade.

The splendid Hospitallers' church of St Mary's can be visited today. Next door stands the thirteenth-century Old Hall, the senior court for the Templars in Warwickshire.

The Hospitallers combined Temple Balsall with their Preceptory of Grafton, later Temple Grafton, on the southern edge of the forest.

By 1470 the Hospitallers had left Temple Balsall and their property was leased to a lay tenant, John Beaufitz. When King Henry VIII suppressed the Order of St John during the Dissolution, Temple Balsall was seized, and in 1543 he gave it to his sixth wife, Katherine Parr.

Queen Elizabeth I awarded Temple Balsall to one of her favourites, Robert Dudley, Earl of Leicester, who lived at Kenilworth Castle. His granddaughter Lady Katherine Leveson of Trentham Hall, Staffordshire, founded an almshouse and school in the village. Their work continues to this day.

The Balsall Shakespeares moved out to nearby Wroxall, Knowle, Packwood and Rowington, their descendants, mainly farming families, spreading further afield to Baddesley Clinton, Lapworth and Snitterfield.

Wroxall, a forest village between Solihull and Warwick, had a small Benedictine convent where, in 1457, an Isabella Shakespeare served as its prioress, as listed in the Register of the Guild of St Anne in the nearby village of Knowle. A nun, Jane Shakespeare, also lived at the convent.

The Balsall Common preceptory of the Knights Templars, now known as the Old Hall.

The ruins of Wroxall Priory, which lie just off the A4141 and can be visited, along with its fourteenth-century church. The later house, Wroxall Abbey, now a hotel and conference centre, became the home of Christopher Wren after he built St Paul's Cathedral.

The entrance to sixteenth-century Packwood House and its magnificent gardens.

The magnificent Packwood yews, shaped to represent the Sermon on the Mount.

The Shakespeares who settled at Packwood, a tiny village to the south of Knowle, later became business partners of William Shakespeare's father John.

Packwood House, a manor whose grounds are bisected by a public road which is a sheer delight to drive through, is now in the care of the National Trust. It is renowned for its garden of yew trees first planted in the eighteenth century, and clipped to represent the Sermon on the Mount.

The first house to stand at Packwood was a timber-framed structure built by John Fetherstone between 1556–60. It became merged into the main part of the later house, which was improved by sixteenth-century pointed gables, mullioned windows and towering chimneystacks.

The great Elizabethan historian Raphael Holinshed lived at Packwood House. He was the author of the *Chronicles of England*, a major source for Shakespeare's historical plays like *Macbeth*. Indeed, the young William Shakespeare may have met him at Packwood on one or more occasions.

In 1642, during the English Civil War, Parliamentarian general Henry Ireton sought hospitality there on the night before the Battle of Edgehill.

However, the careful Fetherstones kept their options open, and legends say that the future Charles II was received at Packwood after losing the Battle of Worcester in 1651.

In the late nineteenth century, the last of the Fetherstones sold the house to George Oakes Arton, and in 1906 it passed into the ownership of business magnate Alfred Ash.

His son, Graham Baron Ash, later High Sheriff of Warwickshire, fell in love with Packwood and began an ambitious restoration project to take the house back to its Tudor heyday. In 1941, he gave the house, its land and contents to the National Trust in memory of his parents.

Another member of the Royal Family visited Packwood. In August 1927, Queen Mary, the wife of King George V, took tea there.

However, let us return to the story of Shakespeare's ancestors.

The first reference to the village of Knowle, now part of Solihull, came in 1200, when William de Arden gave the portion of Hampton parish then known as Gnolle, Saxon for 'small hill', to his wife Amice.

By 1220, the de Ardens built a manor house there, complete with private chapel, while the ordinary folk of Gnolle had to walk five miles to Hampton to attend church, crossing a treacherous ford of the flood-prone River Blythe.

This was the same de Arden family that included ancestors of Mary Arden, the mother of William Shakespeare.

Walter Cook, a clergyman born in Knowle around 1365, gave his home village a church of its own in 1403, and then in 1413 built the magnificent half-timbered Guild House next door. His guild attracted large numbers of wealthy members . . . including a Thomas Shakespeare of Balsall in 1486.

Incidentally, Knowle was the birthplace on 10 July 1903 of another Arden literary figure, the twentieth century science fiction writer John Wyndham Parkes Lucas Beynon Harris, who wrote under the pen name John Wyndham. His novels include *The Day of the Triffids*, *The Kraken Wakes*, *The Chrysalids*, *The Midwich Cuckoos*, and *Trouble with Lichen*. He died in 1969.

Another branch of the Shakespeare family lived in Rowington, an Arden village between Warwick and Henley-in-Arden, and had their home at the appropriately-named half-timbered Shakespeare Hall.

Although this property is not open to the public, the Heart of England Way, a long-distance footpath, runs within sight of it, and leads to the magnificent moated manor house of Baddesley Clinton.

Sundials are a prominent feature of Packwood House.

Knowle's Millennium sign depicts its church, Guild House, its location on the Grand Union Canal and the trees of Arden. Knowle started out as a forest clearing but is now, like its modern sister Dorridge, a major commuter settlement.

Knowle's Guild House and parish church, dedicated to St John the Baptist, St Lawrence the Martyr and St Anne. The church was built of white Arden sandstone from a quarry in Rowington.

Private Shakespeare Hall, home of a branch of the playwright's family, stands at the end of a tree-lined drive in Rowington. Local legends says that he wrote As You Like It *here. William Shakespeare himself owned property in Rowington, a village on the road between Knowle and Warwick. He left a cottage and land in Rowington to his daughter Susanna.*

Chester House in High Street, now Knowle Library, was originally two dwellings built around 1400 and 1500 and is now Grade II listed.*

Historians believe that Adam Shakespeare, recorded as a tenant of land at Baddesley Clinton, was the great-great-grandfather of William Shakespeare.

The playwright's grandfather Richard Shakespeare was born in nearby Wroxall around 1500, and moved from Budbrooke near Warwick to a farm in Snitterfield – leasing land in Bell Lane near the church from none other than the Arden family of Wilmcote for a period of 35 years.

Copies of records referring to the Shakespeare family in the late 16th century are displayed inside Snitterfield parish church.

Richard's younger son John, who was born in 1531 and grew up at the Snitterfield farm, and fell in love with Mary, the youngest of eight daughters of Robert Arden.

Robert, who lived at Glebe Farm, Wilmcote, three miles north of Stratford, was a member of the powerful branch of the Ardens who owned the now-demolished Park Hall at Castle Bromwich near Birmingham.

In 1557, John Shakespeare, aged 26, married Mary, then just 17, in the church of St John the Baptist in Aston Cantlow, the parish church for Wilmcote, the bride's home.

The wedding took place a year after the death of her father, who may not have approved of Mary marrying 'beneath' her, to one of his mere tenants.

The thirteenth-century parish church of St John the Baptist at Aston Cantlow.

Snitterfield parish church of St James the Great has records of the Shakespeare family.

Her father had left her Asbies, the Arden estate in Wilmcote, so she was quite a catch for John.

Here arose an historical conundrum. In 2000, historian Dr Nat Alcock rediscovered deeds and church records which proved that Shakespeare's mother grew up not in the half-timbered Wilmcote house that had been the subject of many generations of postcards, souvenirs, guidebooks and travel articles, but at adjacent Glebe Farm.

The blame for the misidentification lies with notorious Stratford 'historian' John Jordan, who in the late eighteenth century joined others cashing in on the growing popularity of Shakespeare by coming up with all sorts of colourful tales about him, as well as forgeries.

The Shakespeare Birthplace Trust was placed on a legal footing by a private Act of Parliament in 1891, charged with the duty of purchasing "as and when the opportunity shall arise the house at Wilmcote known as the house of Mary Arden his mother."

Although Jordan's claims about the former occupant of the Wilmcote house were first doubted shortly after they were made, the trust nonetheless bought the house in 1930. After extensive restoration, it was opened to the public.

Arden oak timbers are apparent in the structure of the Cock Horse, a delightful traditional hostelry in Rowington.

Over the years, the trust did tell visitors that it was possible that Mary Arden had not lived in the house, but Dr Alcock finally established that it had really belonged to Adam Palmer, who was a mere acquaintance of the Arden family. Not only that, but it had been built in 1569 – 18 years after Mary Arden had moved to Stratford with John Shakespeare!

So the trust renamed Mary Arden's House as Palmer's Farm, while Glebe Farm – luckily bought by the trust in 1968 to save it from demolition – became the 'new' Mary Arden's House.

Both properties, along with a set of original outbuildings, are now home to a countryside museum and a working rare breeds farm.

After John and Mary Shakespeare moved to Stratford in 1551 and John began trading in animals, wool, malt and corn, he set up business both as a glover and as a whittawer (a maker of saddles and harness) and bought a house in Henley Street because it was convenient for the town market.

By sharp contrast with his future eldest son, John had no literary leanings whatsoever: in fact, he could not even write, and used glovers' compasses as his signature! His wife signed her name with the image of a running horse.

Despite his literacy shortcomings, John Shakespeare prospered in Stratford to the point that he was able to buy a second house, in Greenhill Street, in 1552. He held several important positions in the town over two decades, ranging from borough ale taster to bailiff, the highest public office in the town.

The couple had eight children. The first, Joan, born in 1558, died from bubonic plague after two months, and the second, Margaret, born 1562, died aged just five months, it was believed, and possibly from the same disease.

The Shakespeares ran a far higher risk of catching the disease than most of the other 1500 inhabitants of the market town, which then had around 200 houses. Not realised at the time, the plague was passed by fleas living in animal hides, which John Shakespeare regularly dealt in.

On 26 April 1564, the baptismal register of Holy Trinity church in Stratford recorded in Latin, the name of the Shakespeares' third child, Gulielmus Filius Johannes Shakespeare, meaning William, son of John Shakespeare.

Palmer's Farm in Wilmcote, wrongly believed to have been the home of Mary Arden.

In those days, actual birthdays were not registered, although the Book of Common Prayer demanded that a child be baptised on the nearest Sunday or holy day following birth. It was also practice for infants to be baptised three days after birth, because in an era when plague and pestilence were rife, life expectancy remained low. Therefore William Shakespeare's birthday is traditionally held to be 23 April, the feast day of St George, patron saint of England.

Until the late eighteenth century, both of his parents' houses in Stratford claimed to be Shakespeare's birthplace. The problem was solved when one was pulled down, leaving the existing building in Henley Street as the only contender.

John's downfall began in 1570, when he was accused of usury – lending money at far too high a rate of interest. That year, his application for a coat-of-arms and for the title of Gentleman failed – possibly because of his family's (and that of his wife's) Catholic faith at a time of religious strife.

In 1578 John fell into arrears with his taxes, and the following year was forced to mortgage Asbies.

The Mary Arden, a pub in Wilmcote.

The Elizabethan gardens at the rear of Shakespeare's birthplace in Henley Street, Stratford.

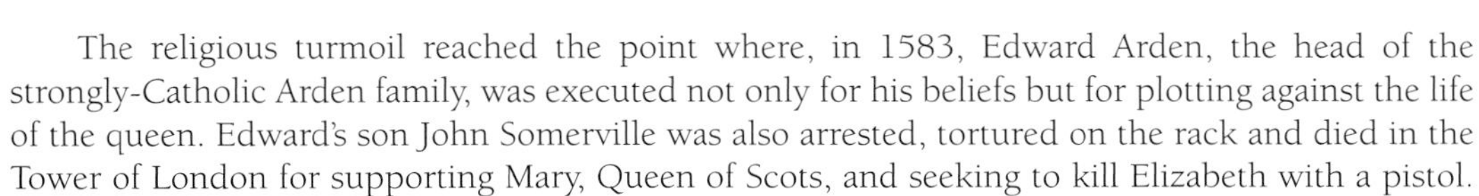

The religious turmoil reached the point where, in 1583, Edward Arden, the head of the strongly-Catholic Arden family, was executed not only for his beliefs but for plotting against the life of the queen. Edward's son John Somerville was also arrested, tortured on the rack and died in the Tower of London for supporting Mary, Queen of Scots, and seeking to kill Elizabeth with a pistol.

Amidst this background of religious strife, John Shakespeare was removed from Stratford's Board of Aldermen, a type of town council, in 1586, and four years later he was left with only his Henley Street house.

It would be left to his famous son William to restore him to favour, thanks to the royal patronage he earned through his success on the London stage.

Accordingly, on 20 October 1596, John Shakespeare (along with his children) was finally granted permission to display the coat-of-arms he had desired for so long, and three years later, he was back on Stratford's town council.

The coat-of-arms was gold with a black banner bearing a silver spear, and a motto, *non sans droit*, meaning "not without right". On top of the banner was a helmet on which stood a falcon holding another spear in its claw, shaking it.

John Shakespeare died in 1601 and his wife seven years later. Overall, John's life had been reasonably happy and successful.

Yet one question will always confound historians and critics alike: how did a son of a small-town merchant who left school at 14 become the world's greatest dramatist? Several critics have doubted that William Shakespeare wrote the plays, and have laid them at the door of more learned Elizabethan figures like the scientist Francis Bacon. Most others, however, believe that Stratford produced a genius.

The room in which William Shakespeare was said to have been born, from an 1880s' photograph.
ROBIN JONES COLLECTION

8

FROM POACHER TO PLAYWRIGHT

Shottery, Temple Grafton, Billesley, Charlecote, Hampton Lucy

The Shakespeares may well have been low in the literacy stakes, but they made sure that young William would not follow in those footsteps. John Shakespeare's election as an Alderman in Stratford-upon-Avon brought the perk of free education for his sons with it. Not so for his daughters, for in those times it was not considered necessary to educate girls.

From the age of seven, William would have likely attended Stratford's King Edward IV Grammar School. Also known as the King's New School, it was founded via a charter by King Edward VI in 1553. Young William would have learned Latin and maybe Greek, and studied great classical authors and dramatists like Ovid, Horace, Virgil, Seneca and Cicero. The school's staff included many Oxford graduates.

Studies would begin at six in the morning and finish at five in the evening in summer, with an hour being cut off at either end of the day in winter. The school week was spread over five-and-a-half days, and pupils also had to attend church services every Sunday.

Lessons consisted of 'cramming' – the constant repetition of subjects – with endless examinations to make certain that the facts had sunk in.

Shakespeare summed up school life:

> *. . . the whining schoolboy, with his satchel*
> *And shining morning face, creeping like a snail*
> *Unwillingly to school . . .* (*As You Like It*, Act 2, Scene 7)

Playwright Ben Jonson, a highly-learned scholar, later described Shakespeare as having "small Latine and lesse Greeke." However, the blame for his supposedly scant knowledge of these subjects may be the result of him leaving school at 14 to help with John's then-shaky business.

Opposite: *Stratford-upon-Avon's King Edward VI School and the adjacent fifteenth-century Guild Chapel. The school moved into the first floor of the half-timbered Guildhall in 1553, and Shakespeare probably attended classes there. At the Guildhall, he would have seen the plays performed by troupes of travelling actors.* ROBIN JONES

John Shakespeare, father of William, is remembered by this stained glass window in the Guild Chapel.

Young William first took centre stage in Stratford not as a famous playwright or actor, but as the subject of a scandal.

Aged 18, he told his shocked parents that he had made a woman eight years older pregnant.

A marriage to the lady, Anne Hathaway, was hastily arranged to stifle the gossip and shame.

Anne was one of eight children of yeoman farmer Richard Hathaway, who lived at Hewland Farm in Shottery, a village a mile from the centre of Stratford, and now a suburb of the town. When Richard Hathaway died in September 1581, he left Anne £6 13s 4d "atte the day of her maryage."

It is not known how Anne met young William, but the romance immortalised Shottery, which once stood on the edge of the forest, and made Hewlands Farm, now known as Anne Hathaway's House, the most famous thatched cottage in the world.

Dating from the 1460s, by the standards of Elizabethan times it was a substantial residence. It remained in the Hathaway family for several generations, although the male line became extinct in 1746 when John Hathaway died.

His sister Susanna passed it to his nephew, John Hathaway Taylor, whose son, William Taylor, lived there until his death in 1846, six years after he sold it to pay off debts but remained a sitting tenant.

His daughter Mary Baker was still living in the house in 1892 when it was bought by the Shakespeare Birthplace Trust along with family heirlooms, including the Hathaway Bed which dates from Anne's time. Maintaining an unbroken link with Anne, Mary was appointed its first custodian, and died in 1899.

Returning to the marriage, a special licence was issued by the Bishop of Worcester on 27 November 1582, and to speed up proceedings, the banns were only read once, instead of the usual three times.

It is believed that the couple wed in the village of Temple Grafton, at a church with links to the Knights Hospitallers, who held the estate here in 1189.

It is not known exactly when the marriage took place – some say 2 December, others 29 November.

Two different entries in the Episcopal Register at Worcester, on 27 November 1582 and 28 November 1582, refer, respectively, to the marriages of "Wm Shaxpere et Annam Whateley de Temple Grafton" and "William Shagspeare and Anne Hathwey." They may record the same event, with "Whately" being a misreading of Hathaway.

Despite the village name, no records survive here of the Hospitallers' predecessors, the Knights Templars, having owned this manor, despite the addition of their name to the Saxon 'Grafton', meaning 'farm by the pit or trench.' There has been a church here since Saxon times, but the present building, which has both a Templar and a Hospitaller portrayed in stained glass windows, dates from 1875.

Temple Grafton's twin village is Ardens Grafton, named around 1200, again after the great Norman family whose name was synonymous with the forest and were also ancestors of Shakespeare's mother. Temple Grafton is immortalised in a traditional local rhyme often and almost certainly wrongly attributed to Shakespeare:

> *Piping Pebworth, Dancing Marston, Haunted Hillboro', Hungry Grafton, Dodging Exhall, Papist Wixford, Beggarly Broom and Drunken Bidford . . .*

However, you would not go hungry in Grafton today.

At the crossroads between the village and neighbouring Binton stands the Blue Boar public house, restaurant and hotel, which has the distinctive feature of a well in the bar floor covered by a thick glass plate with goldfish swimming beneath.

For years there was also a small plaque in the bar subtly claiming a Shakespearean connection, but the management made a song and dance about it. Yet if William did marry Anne at Temple Grafton, surely it was likely that guests may have called in for a pint or three on the way back to Stratford?

It has also been suggested that because of the Shakespeares' Catholicism, the couple were privately married by a papist priest in the oratory of Shottery manor house, but no evidence supports this.

The 'lost' Arden village of Billesley a mile to the east has also staked its claim as the place where the couple wed. The tiny church, which has some twelfth century stonework, is also held to have been the place where the playwright's granddaughter Elizabeth Nash married John Barnard in the 1640s. We will never know for certain, because all the records prior to 1816 have been lost.

The courting settle inside Anne Hathaway's cottage, from an early twentieth-century hand-coloured postcard.

The Blue Boar, Temple Grafton's ancient crossroads hostelry, which Shakespeare's wedding guests may have visited.

This nineteenth-century church at Temple Grafton replaced the earlier one where William Shakespeare's hurried wedding to Anne Hathaway is believed to have taken place.

Billesley also harks from Saxon times, when it was 'Bill's clearing' in the great forest. The *Domesday Book* records a large peasant population, but the Black Death, poor harvests and the eviction of large numbers of the population to make way for sheep grazing brought about its demise. By the late fifteenth century, only the church and manor house survived.

The Trussell family held the Billesley estate until 1588, when Thomas Trussell was hanged for felony on the highway. It then passed to the crown. The manor house was rebuilt in the seventeenth century and is now a luxury hotel. A local tale claims that Shakespeare wrote *As You Like It* there.

The parish of Billesley was merged with Wilmcote in 1955, and the church, rebuilt in 1692, was declared redundant in 1976. It remains consecrated, maintained by the Churches Conservation Trust, and is still occasionally used for worship.

Local tradition holds that William Shakespeare and Anne Hathaway married in this delightful little church at Billesley, rather than at nearby Temple Grafton as generally accepted.

Billesley Manor is now a luxury hotel.

It is believed that the newly-married couple moved in with John and Mary Shakespeare, and in May 1583, their daughter Susanna was born.

At this time, William probably continued to help out with his father's businesses, and may have undertaken some teaching, as well as work with a lawyer. His father was also a moneylender, and his son picked up the tricks of the trade, for William loaned sums of money when he later lived in London.

William and Anne subsequently had twins, Hamnet and Judith, in 1585. Hamnet died at the age of 11, possibly from the plague.

Next to nothing is known about William Shakespeare between 1585 and 1592, yet his plays display a far greater knowledge of the world that he would likely have learned at Stratford's grammar school, leading to speculation he may have travelled abroad. Indeed, several of his plays are set in Italy – *Romeo and Juliet, The Merchant of Venice, The Two Gentlemen of Verona.*

We know he had moved to London by 1592, but we do not know exactly why.

Was he fed up of married life, or did harsh treatment from a merciless magistrate cause him to run away from Stratford?

A well-told traditional tale, for which there exists no documentary proof, relates that Shakespeare was caught poaching deer on the estate of Sir Thomas Lucy, a local Justice of the Peace and the builder of magnificent Charlecote Park, which lies on the River Avon between Stratford and Warwick.

Lucy humiliated him and ordered him to be whipped, so the tale goes.

It was said that Shakespeare was so annoyed at his treatment that he wrote a verse which he hung on Lucy's gate:

A parliament member,
a justice of peace,
At home a poor scarecrow,
at London an asse,
If lowsie is Lucy,
as some volke miscalle it,
Then Lucy is lowsie,
whatever befall it.
He thinks himself great;
Yet an asse in his state,
We allow, by his ears,
but with asses to mate,
if Lucy is lowsie,
as some volke miscall it,
Then sing lowsie Lucy whatever befall it.

A Charles Cattermole watercolour depicting the young William Shakespeare's hearing before Thomas Lucy at Charlecote for deer poaching.

Lucy was said to have been so angered by the verse that he applied to the County Attorney for Shakespeare's arrest, which was duly signed, tradition has it, on the Elizabethan table now in St Mary's Guildhall, Coventry – causing the young man to flee Stratford to avoid further punishment.

Shakespeare exacted further revenge on Lucy by parodying him as the Cotswold magistrate Justice Shallow in *The Merry Wives of Windsor* and *Henry IV Part 2.*

The Lucy family certainly believed that their ancestor's character had been lampooned as Shallow, and had the relevant pages from their copies of Shakespeare's complete works removed.

And although the deer herds for which Charlecote Park, now in the care of the National Trust, is famous were not established until the 1840s, the surrounding estates would have been filled with wild deer in Shakespeare's day.

The great Elizabethan gatehouse to Charlecote Manor has survived from Shakespeare's day.

Like the Ardens, the Lucys came to England with William the Conqueror, and inherited the manor of Charlecote in 1247.

Thomas Lucy was knighted at Charlecote in 1565 by Robert Dudley, Earl of Leicester, deputising for Queen Elizabeth I. Her majesty, however, visited Charlecote seven years afterwards, spending two nights in the Great Bedchamber, now the Drawing Room. The sixteenth-century Renaissance porch at the entrance front of the house features the arms of Elizabeth, marking her visit.

The east front of the house still retains much of its Elizabethan form, with gables and octagonal corner turrets, each with their own cupola, ball and weathervane.

Bachelor George Lucy employed Capability Brown to landscape the 188 acres of grounds around 1760, when Jacob sheep were introduced.

It is reputed that Horatio Nelson once slept in the Ebony Bedroom in the house.

The gatehouse is the only original Elizabethan feature to survive intact. Although the general outline of the Elizabethan house remains, most of it is now Victorian.

The house and park, which are both open to the public, is still the home of the Lucys. Their name is also remembered in the sister parish and village of Hampton Lucy, which has retained its charm as a real backwater of rural Britain of times past.

This village was recorded in 781 when, Offa, King of Mercia, gave 17 hides of land in Hampton – Saxon for 'farm in the water meadows' – to the Bishop of Worcester. It was known as Bishop's Hampton, or Busshopeshampton, until 1549, when the manor was sold to John Dudley, Duke of Northumberland.

Hampton is divided from Charlecote by the River Avon, and travellers passed between the two via an ancient ford which became treacherous in winter. A church was believed to have been built at Hampton in the 1200s.

In 1555, the Protestant Dudley was executed on the orders of Queen Mary, and on 12 June 1557, she leased the manor to Thomas Lucy.

The English Civil War brought misery to Hampton Lucy, when a parliamentary army billeted there in 1642 plundered the church and village for firewood prior to the battle of Edge Hill on 23 October.

The parish church of St Peter was built on the site of the medieval church in 1826. Designed by Thomas Rickman, it was funded by the Reverend John Lucy, who preached there for nearly 60 years.

The iron bridge over the Avon was supplied in 1829 by Horseley Ironworks in Ironbridge. Shropshire, the cradle of the Industrial Revolution, and where the world's first iron bridge proudly stands above the Severn Gorge.

One of the most famous sons of Hampton Lucy is Charles Maries, the great Victorian plant collector (1851–1902), who learned botany in the village.

Employed by the Chelsea nurseryman Sir Harry Veitch to collect species in Japan and China between 1877–79, three years later Maries became Superintendent of Gardens to the Maharajah of Durbhungah in India.

He introduced many exotic species to Britain for the first time, including the Japanese banana. The Maries Fir, a conifer native to Japan, was named in his honour after he brought it to Britain in 1879.

His manuscripts are in the archives at Kew Gardens.

Proud villagers have set up a trail highlighting plants introduced by Maries.

However, the principal attraction for visitors today is Charlecote Mill, which was built in 1806 and stands on the site of earlier water mills, at least one operated in Saxon times.

The existing mill and house were built by the Lucy estate, and are still owned by Sir Edmund Fairfax Lucy. It was restored to working order in 1978, and featured in a BBC TV production of George Eliot's *The Mill on the Floss,* and is open on selected days.

Whether or not Lucy's punishment was to blame, there must have been a compelling reason for William Shakespeare to flee to London, and to adopt one of the most despised professions of the day, acting.

Yet was the prospect of a stage career the true motive after all ?

Acting troupes played in Stratford during his formative years, and John Shakespeare's civic duties would have included issuing them with the necessary licenses. His son may have known some of these travelling actors and become fascinated with their lifestyle.

In 1592, William Shakespeare was not only working in London, but Lord Strange's Men were performing his *Henry VI Part 1* at the Rose Theatre.

The wheel of fortune had clearly turned for this troupe, for when they previously visited Stratford on 11 February 1579, the town's corporation was unimpressed by the performance and gave them only five shillings.

The church of St Peter ad Vincula in Hampton Lucy, built from Cotswold stone. Many windows were blown out by an explosion when a fully-laden bomber crashed during the Second World War.

PRINCESS MARINA

9
STRATFORD-UPON-AVON

The town and playwright that made each other

Throughout the course of history, Shakespeare has enjoyed a symbiotic relationship with his home town. Yes, he did not make his fame and fortune in this southern outpost of Arden, but it was an event in Stratford that 150 years after his death that springboarded him towards the dizzy heights of the immortal fame that he enjoys today.

Opposite: *One of many pleasure boats on the Avon at Stratford crosses the path of the town's historic ferry.*

In turn, that same fame made Stratford the second most popular destination for overseas visitors after London.The earliest record of Stretforde, the Saxon 'straet' referring to a Roman road, and ford, to a river crossing, came in 691.

It had been a key crossing point in Roman times, and probably before, since the times when ancient British settlers made their home on the edge of the forest.

It would have been a major trading centre for the heart of England. A Roman road ran from the river crossing to the Fosse Way and Banbury in one direction, and the town of Alauna (Alcester) in the other.

Stretforde took a giant stride forward in 1196 when the Bishop of Worcester, John de Coutances, turned his estates there into a new town.

The bishop obtained a weekly market charter from Richard I and gave his tenants the right to rent quarter-acre development plots or 'burgages'. Unlike their country cousins who laboured under the Norman feudal system and were tied to their lord's manor, the 'burgesses' could trade freely.

So Stratford became a town of tradesmen and merchants, who established the Guild of the Holy Cross, a body which handled matters of family welfare and education for their sons as well as religious and commercial interests.

Sir Hugh Clopton, a London mercer and Lord Mayor during the reign of Henry VII, replaced the dilapidated wooden bridge across the Avon with an infinitely sturdier structure comprising "14 great arches of stone and long cawsey". Known as Clopton Bridge, it carries today's heavy road traffic on the A3400.

The Royal Shakespeare Theatre at Stratford illuminating the River Avon at night.

Holy Trinity church keeps a watchful eye over the River Avon.

Clopton also enlarged and restored Stratford's Holy Trinity parish church and the Guild Chapel, paved roads for the first time – and erected the second biggest house in the town, New Place in Church Street.

While William Shakespeare made his fortune in London, his wife and children remained in Stratford. The playwright bought New Place in Chapel Street for £60 in 1597, when he was at the height of his career.

That purchase established him as a townsman of Stratford, like his father. He finally settled at New Place in 1610.

Shakespeare died on 23 April 1616 at the age of 52 give or take a day or two, reputedly after a visit to the Bell Inn at Welford-on-Avon with fellow writers Ben Jonson and Michael Drayton, after which he trudged the four miles back home in a downpour which left him with pneumonia.

New Place was left to his daughter Susanna Hall, who once entertained Charles I's queen, Henrietta, there. Susanna left the house to her daughter Elizabeth, who married Thomas Nash, owner of the sixteenth-century half-timbered Nash's House next door. It is believed that Anne Hathaway probably saw out her last days at New Place, passing away in 1623.

The stone spire of Holy Trinity church was added after Shakespeare's day.

Clopton Bridge, which has served Stratford well for six centuries.

After Elizabeth Hall died, the house was bought back by the Clopton family.

Sir John Clopton opened it to the public – and in doing so became an early advocate of tourism in Stratford.

However, the next owner of the house, the Reverend Francis Gastrell, became so fed up with tourists that one night in 1759, he ripped out a mulberry tree in the garden said to be planted by Shakespeare, and chopped it up into logs. Townsfolk were furious and smashed his windows.

Gastrell, sadly, was not finished. Faced with a Land Tax bill, he had New Place demolished. All that survives are its foundations.

For this deed, Gastrell was driven out of town.

Visitors to the site of New Place – accessed through Nash's House – can access the adjacent Elizabethan-style knott garden and Shakespeare's Great Garden with its colourful flowerbeds and mulberry tree, said to be grown from a cutting of the original.

Nash's House now houses Stratford's local history museum, with many items of Jacobean and Tudor furniture on display.

By far the biggest turning point in the fortunes of both Stratford and its greatest son came in 1769, when renowned London actor David Garrick organised a Shakespeare Jubilee festival in the town.

All that remains of New Place, Shakespeare's retirement home, are these foundations.

The front of Nash's House in Chapel Street

This landmark event has been hailed as the "point at which Shakespeare stopped being regarded as an increasingly popular and admirable dramatist, and became a god," while others regarded it as little better than a circus which ended up having scant relevance to Shakespeare's work.

Seven years before the Jubilee, Stratford had become a destination for the growing number of admirers of the playwright's work, and local merchant Thomas Sharpe sold trinkets said to have been carved from the wood of the ill-fated mulberry.

In 1767, Stratford's corporation could not afford to repair the town hall, and decided to use the Shakespeare connection to entice the London theatrical community who might be able to help.

Garrick was approached, and quickly saw the full extent of the commercial possibilities.

The town hall was rebuilt in 1768 with his input, and Garrick presented a statue of Shakespeare to be displayed there. As a reward, he was formally elected the first Freeman of the Borough, and was handed a presentational scroll contained in a small chest made from the mulberry tree wood.

Since his groundbreaking Shakespearean debut as Richard III in 1741, Garrick had revolutionised the stage presentation of the playwright's works with a never-before-seen degree of realism and naturalism. Numerous theatregoers 'discovered' Shakespeare for the first time through Garrick.

He generated an unprecedented wave of publicity for his Jubilee festival. Souvenirs were turned out en masse not only for the big three-day event in September 1769, but as a result of its impact, ever afterwards for over two centuries of visitors who would make their pilgrimages to the Bard's home town.

Crowds poured into Stratford like never before. However, after two days of solid rain, the Jubilee was a washout. Garrick cancelled it on the third day amidst scenes of chaos.

The massive Tudor Grade I listed Shakespeare Hotel in Church Street has, reputedly at actor David Garrick's suggestion, 86 rooms each named after a character from a Shakespeare play.

The Jubilee's saving grace was Garrick's own performance of his *Ode upon dedicating a building and, erecting a statue, to Shakespeare, at Stratford-upon-Avon*, which took place inside a rotunda he had built in honour of Shakespeare.

It was the greatest performance of Garrick's life and inspired many subsequent poems, articles, and plays in its own right for years afterwards.

The Jubilee lifted the mere appreciation of Shakespeare into a cult, with Stratford at its hub. It expanded Shakespeare's appeal from the elitist confines of the literary and scholastic world to a mass-market audience: ordinary people who had never seen or read one of his plays were suddenly clamouring to know all about him, his life story and the places where he lived.

Today's Shakespeare's birthday celebrations, a direct successor to the Jubilee, take place annually, on the weekend closest to 23 April.

The Great Western Railway finally reached Stratford in 1860, greatly boosting it as a mass daytrip destination, crowds from the industrial conurbations of Birmingham and Coventry pouring in for the annual Shakespeare Birthday Weekend, the town regatta, fairs and Bank Holidays and outings on the river.

The Gower Memorial statue of Shakespeare in Bancroft Gardens. The statue, showing Shakespeare seated, is flanked by life-size statues of Lady Macbeth, Hamlet, Prince Hal and Falstaff, representing philosophy, tragedy, history, and comedy and was presented by Lord Ronald Sutherland-Gower, to the town in 1888.

Shakespeare's portrait in mosaic above the entrance to the Old Bank, which dates from 1810.

The statue of Lady Macbeth.

In 1833, Edward Fordham Flower founded a brewery, Flowers (later bought by Whitbread), which became one of Stratford's biggest employers. Afterwards the Flower family began to buy up parcels of land along the riverbank.

In 1875, Charles Flower gave two acres of land alongside the river and £1000 to launch an international campaign to build a Shakespeare Memorial Theatre. He also created the Bancroft pleasure gardens alongside the canal basin, while his brother Edgar restored the old grammar school buildings in the 1890s.

Four years later, in his role as mayor on the anniversary of Shakespeare's birthday, he formally opened a beautiful Victorian Gothic playhouse of intricate brickwork and castle features, designed by William Frederick Unsworth, with *Much Ado About Nothing* the first play performed there.

The first season at the Shakespeare Memorial Theatre lasted just eight days in the spring, and was not extended until 1910, and then to only a month – hardly a rival to the London theatres of the day.

However, from 1907 star actors began to appear in Stratford such as Ellen Terry and H. Beerbohm Tree, and the Memorial Theatre became so highly regarded that it was granted a Royal Charter in 1925.

However, a tragedy of Shakespearean proportions befell the building a year later, when the theatre was destroyed by fire, leaving just a burned-out-shell.

Thankfully, buildings adjoining the theatre were not seriously damaged. They included the library, which contained around 10,000 volumes of Shakespeare editions and dramatic literature.

The original Shakespeare Memorial Theatre which burned down in 1926.

The Royal Shakespeare Theatre before its remodelling.

Townsfolk backed a worldwide campaign to build a replacement, and architect Elisabeth Scott won a competition in 1928 to design a new theatre. The art deco building was opened by the Prince of Wales on Shakespeare's birthday in 1932 and is now Grade II* listed.

A radical design for the times, it gave Stratford a state-of-the-art theatre and a firm foundation on which to develop the tourist trade. The remaining shell of the old building was incorporated into the new complex as a conference centre and rehearsal rooms.

In 1960, Peter Hall formed the modern Royal Shakespeare Company and in 1961, the Memorial Theatre was renamed the Royal Shakespeare Theatre.

An additional RSC theatre, The Other Place, opened in 1974. In 1986, part of the shell of the original Memorial Theatre was converted by Michael Reardon into the Swan Theatre and Ashcroft Room, a modern facility based on the design of the playhouses of Elizabethan England.

In 2007, the RSC began a £100-million three-year redevelopment of the main Stratford theatre. The plans, drawn up by Rab and Denise Bennetts of Bennetts Associates, include a new 1000-seat auditorium which will bring the audience much closer to the action on stage, improved public spaces, a riverside walkway, new artists' facilities, exhibition spaces, a rooftop restaurant and a tower with a 33-metre high viewing platform.

Visitors for a century or more have delighted in the circular walk along the south bank of the river through the recreation ground, over the footbridge at the western end, and back along the north bank, taking in Holy Trinity parish church and the theatre itself before arriving back at the gardens.

A church alongside the Avon at Stratford was first mentioned in a charter of 845, signed by Beorhtwulf, king of Mercia. The Normans replaced what would have been a basic wooden structure with a stone building.

Today's building, constructed from limestone, may well be the most-visited parish church in England.

Much loved by generations of actors and actresses is the Dirty Duck pub opposite the Royal Shakespeare Theatre.

The £100-million rebuilding of the Royal Shakespeare Theatre in full swing in January 2009, shortly after the 'topping out' ceremony had taken place.

Shakespeare's elder daughter Susanna married Dr John Hall, a medical practitioner who qualified at Cambridge and Montpelier in 1607. The couple set up home in Hall's Croft, the main part of which was erected in 1613.

Started in 1210, it was designed in the shape of a cross and is approached along an avenue of lime trees representing the 12 tribes of Israel and the 12 Apostles.

Between 1280 and 1330, the local Guild of the Holy Cross paid for the building of the tower and the rebuilding of the nave with side aisles.

In 1331 John, Bishop of Winchester, founded a chantry for five priests in the Thomas Becket Chapel in the south aisle, and built a stone house to accommodate this College of Priests.

Henry V confirmed the privileges of the College in 1451, but it was suppressed by Henry VIII at the reformation, when its assets were given to the town, its privileges sold off, and much of the interior destroyed.

It is all but certain that Shakespeare worshipped in the church. In 1605, he bought a share of the privileges for £440, giving him the right of burial in the chancel, as happened on 25 April 1616.

In his boyhood a charnel house stood next to the chancel, where the bones of those dug up to make room for new graves could again be laid to rest. Shakespeare did not want to see his body meet this fate, so he followed the common practice of having a curse placed on his grave slab!

The right of burial was inherited by Shakespeare's family after he died. Anne Hathaway, the couple's daughter Susanna, her husband Dr John Hall and Thomas Nash, the first husband of Shakespeare's granddaughter Elizabeth, are buried alongside him.

Within a few years of his death, and before Anne died in 1623, a memorial to Shakespeare was erected inside the chancel. It is thought to be a reasonably accurate likeness.

Each year, on the Saturday closest to St George's Day, the church hosts the Shakespeare's Birthday pageant as thousands march through the town to lay flowers on his grave.

Shakespeare's monument inside the chantry of Holy Trinity church. It is believed to have been commissioned by Shakespeare's daughter Susanna and her husband Dr Hall, and is mentioned in a verse by Leonard Digges in the First Folio of the plays:

> And Time dissolves thy Stratford Monument,
> Here we alive shall view thee soon. This book,
> When brass and marble fade, shall make thee look
> Fresh to all ages.

Mention must be made of another prominent sixteenth-century half-timbered house in the town, the High Street home of John Harvard (1607–38), whose legacy led to the founding of Harvard University in the United States.

Harvard House was rebuilt by butcher and maltster Thomas Rogers after a great fire destroyed many of Stratford's buildings in 1594.

His daughter Katherine became the second wife of butcher Robert Harvard, the couple being married at Holy Trinity Church on 8 April 1605. Their son John was baptised on 29 November 1607 in St Saviour's, Southwark.

In 1625 when John was 18, Robert and four of his children died from the plague, leaving his sons John and Thomas.

John Harvard entered Emmanuel College, Cambridge, in 1627, to pursue a career in the ministry, attaining a Masters degree. Katherine Harvard died in 1636 and left him the Queen's Head tavern in Southwark, and a half share in houses in Barking.

He sold much of his property in 1637 and emigrated to America, where Puritans were not persecuted. He became a freeman of the colony of Charlestown in November 1637 and a teacher at the church there.

However, he died after a short illness in 1638, aged just 31. Half his estate was left to his wife, and the other half and all his library to a proposed new educational establishment for the colony, which became Harvard University.

Cox's Yard, a former timber yard alongside the Avon, is now a fashionable bistro.

The Garrick Inn and Harvard House.

Next door stands the popular Garrick Inn, which dates from the late sixteenth century. It has been an inn since 1718, and received its current name in 1769 in recognition of the Jubilee.

Apart from the annual Shakespeare birthday celebrations, Stratford is also famous for its mop fair. As a major trading centre over the centuries, Stratford held an annual hiring fair on 12 October, to which farmers, tradesmen and householders came to choose servants for the coming year. After the First World War, the Stratford Mop, as it had become known, became a funfair with side shows, rides and roundabouts.

Today, Bridge Street, High Street, Wood Street, Rother Street, Greenhill Street and Meer Street are closed to accommodate the fair.

After the Mayor reads the Proclamation at Market Cross, the Master of the Mop escorts the civic party on an inspection of the fair. The mayor will choose to go on one ride – after which all children from the town may go free of charge for the morning.

The Runaway Mop follows on the Friday after the mop. A cut-down version of the main fair, it gave those servants who did not like their new employment the chance to find another job.

Alternatively, if it had been 1587, they could always have left for London and a career on the stage!

10

BY BOAT THROUGH ARDEN

On the trail of a forgotten transport pioneer

Imagine the scenario if Ben Jonson, not William Shakespeare, had become established as the leading playwright of Elizabethan times.

And what if posterity had raised Jonson's plays and poetry to dizzy heights to the exclusion of the works of his rival and friend from Stratford-upon-Avon?

That may well have ended up being the case, had not Shakespeare's admirers collected together manuscripts and copies of his works together to be published as the First Folio of 1623, seven years after his death.

A twist of fate could easily have seen Shakespeare's works overlooked, and the accolades we today afford to *Macbeth, Hamlet* or *King Lear* might have instead been perpetually showered on *Volpone, The Alchemist* or *Bartholomew's Fair*.

Unlikely? Far fetched?

This is exactly what befell another great – but unheralded – son of Arden, who was born around two centuries later, and pursued a career not in literature but in transport technology.

Several historians now believe that William James, born in Henley-in-Arden in 1771, and not George Stephenson, as popularly believed, was the true father of modern railways.

The concept of the self-powered vehicle as manifested in the steam railway changed the face of the globe, opening up new territories for colonisation and development and allowing goods to be exported and imported cheaply.

Few schoolboys have heard of James, and yet their hands shoot up into the air when asked which engineer built the locomotive *Rocket*.

James was educated at Warwick & Winson School, and like his father, trained as a solicitor and in 1804 was appointed as the Earl of Warwick's land agent.

As his personal fortune grew, he bought a colliery in South Staffordshire and became the first to open a mine in the West Bromwich coalfield, paving a way for the exploitation of the mineral reserves of the Black Country.

Opposite: *Dyer's Lane bridge on the Stratford canal in Illshaw Heath.*

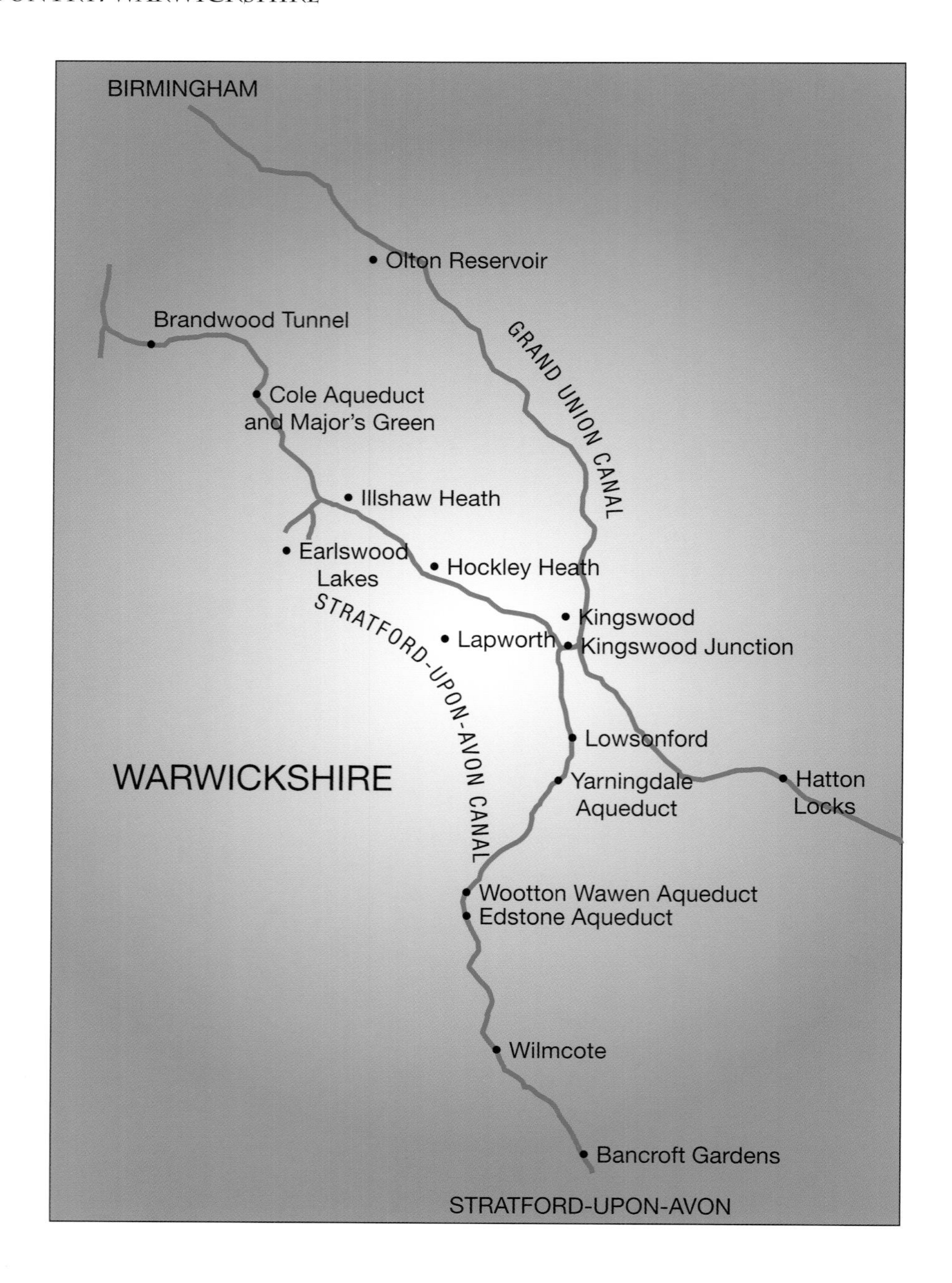
BIRMINGHAM
Olton Reservoir
Brandwood Tunnel
GRAND UNION CANAL
Cole Aqueduct
and Major's Green
Illshaw Heath
Earlswood
Lakes
Hockley Heath
Kingswood
Lapworth
Kingswood Junction
STRATFORD-UPON-AVON CANAL
Lowsonford
WARWICKSHIRE
Yarningdale
Aqueduct
Hatton
Locks
Wootton Wawen Aqueduct
Edstone Aqueduct
Wilmcote
Bancroft Gardens
STRATFORD-UPON-AVON

As a leading proponent of the West Midlands canal system, he became deputy chairman and the major shareholder of the company which built the Stratford-upon-Avon Canal, one of two artificial waterways which bisect the old forest roughly from north to south.

The canal was authorised by an initial Act of Parliament in 1793, and additional Acts in 1795 and 1799. Cutting began in November 1793 at Kings Norton on the Worcester and Birmingham Canal. The completed canal was opened at its junction with the River Avon at Bancroft Basin in Stratford on 24 June 1816.

The canal is 25½ miles long and cost £297,000 to build. Its major engineering features are 56 locks, a 35-yard 16-feet-wide tunnel at Brandwood near King's Norton, a large single-span brick aqueduct over the River Cole at Major's Green near Shirley and three cast-iron trough aqueducts at Yarningale, Wootton Wawen and Edstone (the longest on any canal in Britain), which were the responsibility of James.

There are also three high embankments, the Earlswood Lakes feeder reservoirs and a junction with the Grand Union Canal at Kingswood near Lapworth, which in its heyday, was one of the nation's busiest transport interchanges.

Both canals reached Kingswood through a series of locks which could take boatmen more than a day to pass. To the south, 21 locks lower the Grand Union from Hatton through Warwick, while 19 locks take the Stratford canal from Hockley Heath down to Lapworth.

At the junction, a short quarter-mile length of canal links the two, and a water supply reservoir was created to keep the canals 'topped up'. Around the junction sprang up boatyards, workshops, canal offices and inevitably pubs.

William James' stupendous Edstone Aqueduct near Bearley takes boaters through the treetops of old Arden!

The lock where the Stratford-upon-Avon Canal meets the Avon, with a liberal sprinkling of Stratford's famous swans in attendance.

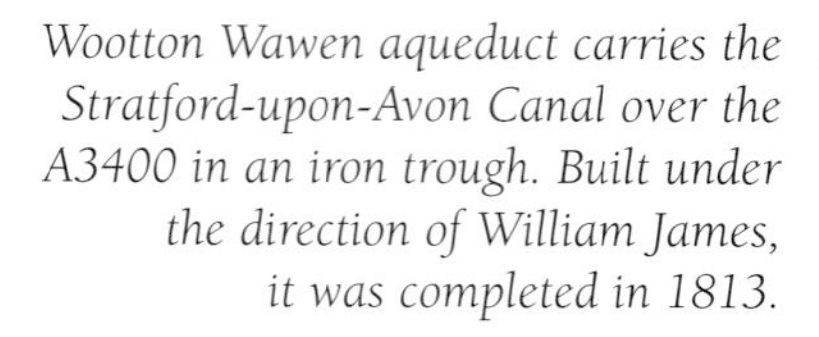

Wootton Wawen aqueduct carries the Stratford-upon-Avon Canal over the A3400 in an iron trough. Built under the direction of William James, it was completed in 1813.

The Grand Union Canal, with a length of 127 miles, is the longest single artificial waterway in Britain and connects London with Birmingham. The section built as the Warwick & Birmingham Canal reached Kingswood around 1799.

With the Earl of Warwick a strong supporter, the Act of Parliament for this canal was passed in March 1793. It authorised a canal from the Digbeth branch of the Birmingham Canal running for 22 miles to Warwick.

From Digbeth the line rose by six Camp Hill Locks, to Bordesley to its summit, which it maintained for some ten miles to Knowle, where there are six falling locks.

From there the canal ran through the 433-yard Shrewley Tunnel to the top of the Hatton flight of locks.

The main water supply is Olton Reservoir, also known as Olton Mere, now leased from British Waterways by a private sailing club.

At Kingswood Junction stands one of six surviving lock keeper's cottages with barrel vaulted roofs, a feature unique to the Stratford canal. They were built during the Napoleonic wars by engineers trained to erect bridges rather than houses and so used the same construction methods for both!

The plaque on Wootton Wawen aqueduct recording James' involvement in the canal.

Traditional canalware as seen at Kingswood Junction.

The massive staircase of locks on the Grand Union Canal at Hatton, with Warwick church on the horizon.

Lapworth originally grew up in an Arden clearing. Its name comes from 'laeppe' meaning 'detached'; in this case, it was a detached part of Kineton Hundred, one of the ancient administrative districts of Warwickshire.

Lapworth is a substantial but scattered settlement: while the shops and railway station, originally known as Kingswood, and the main area of housing for the 2100-strong population are within a stone's throw of the canal junction, its parish church lies more than a mile away.

St Mary the Virgin traces its history back to the tenth century, when a Saxon wattle and wood church stood where the nave now stands.

By 1100, a stone church existed on the site, and was slowly expanded over the next 300 years, and what we see now is, by and large as appearances go, a fifteenth-century church.

James' collieries and the canal made him a rich man and by 1815 he was worth £150,000.

He was also Deputy Recorder for Warwick from 1801, Commandant of the Warwick Defence Volunteers from 1801 to 1804 and remained as land agent to the earl until 1814. He owned much property in Warwick and rented offices in High Street, now covered by the Aylesford restaurant and hotel.

St Mary the Virgin, the parish church of Lapworth, dates back to the tenth century when it was built on high land overlooking the forest, but is a mile away from the canal junction which gives the modern settlement its identity.

Sailing dinghies on Olton Reservoir, which supplies water to the Grand Union Canal.

However, James had far grander visions than the building of a waterway merely to link the Avon with Birmingham and the Black Country.

He saw that the future lay in railways, which until the nineteenth century were little more than short affairs on which horses hauled wagons down to the nearest navigable waterway or harbour.

The first successful public demonstration of a steam locomotive by Richard Trevithick and its at Penydarren near Merthyr Tydfil in 1804, and the subsequent development of the concept by engineers in the coalfields of north-east England in the ensuing decade changed all that.

James had the vision of Stratford's Bancroft Basin as the hub of a major nationwide transport system.

He drew up ambitious plans for a horse-drawn railway linking the canal basin to London via Moreton-in-Marsh, Oxford, Thame and Uxbridge, to transport products from the Black Country to the capital – and although the mode of transport had still not caught on by then, he dared to suggest, once his survey for the ambitious route was completed in 1820, that it would use steam locomotives.

James met George Stephenson at Killingworth Colliery in 1821. The pair agreed to build what would have been the world's first inter-city railway, between Liverpool and Hull, but were unable to get the project off the ground.

Bancroft Basin today accommodates a multitude of narrowboats for pleasure cruising. In 2008/9 much of the gardens were relandscaped.

James had yet more railway plans up his sleeve, this time for a line linking Liverpool to Manchester, after having suggested building a line between the two cities as early as 1803.

He received the backing of wealthy Quaker merchant Joseph Sanders, and also drew up plans for many other railways around Britain.

However, he quickly found that while many ears were listening to him, the sky was not the limit as far as finance was concerned – and in 1823, James was bankrupted and imprisoned for debt.

In his absence, Sanders formed the Liverpool & Manchester Railway Company – and invited Stephenson to produce a new survey. And it was Stephenson's report, not that which James produced four years earlier, which in 1826 impressed Parliament sufficiently to sanction the building of that line.

After release from prison, James retired to Cornwall, still drawing up plans for railways which, sadly, were never built.

He died there penniless and in obscurity in 1837, eight years after Stephenson's *Rocket* won the Rainhill Trials of 1829.

Thanks to a jailer's key, the fame and the glory many now believe was rightfully due to James therefore went to Stephenson.

James' 'own' railway opened on 5 September 1826, in the form of the Stratford & Moreton Tramway.

Tramway Bridge, the biggest surviving artefact from the Stratford & Moreton Tramway, which would have linked the West Midlands to London had William James' dream been realised.

It did serve Bancroft Basin, but never reached London, as only the first 16 miles between Stratford and Moreton-in-Marsh were ever built, and no steam locomotives ever ran on it. Technology passed it by, and it relied throughout its existence on horses to pull the trains, until it fell into disuse by 1902, its rails finally being ripped up for the war effort in 1918.

Its finest legacy is Tramway Bridge in the heart of Stratford, and one of the horse-drawn wagons has been restored and stands nearby.

In recent years, efforts have been made to resurrect James' historical standing.

A commemorative plaque has been installed on the wall of Yew Tree House, the sixteenth-century Henley property where he and his wife spent the early years of their marriage. The couple sold it in 1802 when they moved to Wellesbourne.

Trade on the Stratford Canal reached its peak in 1838, but afterwards declined with the advent of the railways.

The Stratford Canal company sold out to the Oxford, Worcester & Wolverhampton Railway in 1856. Ownership passed to the Great Western Railway in 1865 and to British Waterways following nationalisation in 1948, but by then, the southern section from Kingswood to Stratford was all but derelict, and the northern section from King's Norton Junction was blocked when Lifford Bridge was repaired by the Great Western in such a way that it could not be opened by boaters.

The commemorative plaque on Yew Tree House.

This beautiful cross section of old Arden was nearly lost forever, but for a handful of campaigners over the next decade.

Canal supporter Lord Methuen raised the issue in the House of Lords in 1947, and was assured that the bridge "would be lifted at any time on notice of intended passage being given."

Author Tom Rolt of the Inland Waterways Association, the man who started the British heritage railway movement when his band of volunteers saved the Talyllyn Railway in central Wales, duly gave notice that he intended to pass under the bridge on 20 May 1947, and succeeded in doing so.

The battle was far from won, for in 1958, Warwickshire County Council applied for a warrant of abandonment so that it could repair a road bridge at Wilmcote cheaply. Had the repairs gone ahead, the bridge would have become impassible and the canal would have closed.

Members of the nascent Stratford-upon-Avon Canal Society successfully thwarted this closure bid by producing two licences which proved that navigation of the canal had been made within three years of the council's notice of abandonment.

Working in conjunction with the Inland Waterways Association and the Coventry Canal Society, the Stratford-upon-Avon Canal Society enlisted the support of the National Trust which acquired the southern section of the canal.

The unique Stratford-upon-Avon Canal barrel-roofed lock cottage at Lowsonford.

The house in High Street, Henley, where James lived, was originally known as Yew Tree Hall because of eight trees in the garden planted in the early eighteenth century.

Volunteers from the Boy Scouts, the armed services and even prisoners from Winson Green prison, restored the southern section from Kingswood Junction to Stratford between 1961 and 1964. The section was reopened to navigation on 11 July 1964 by the Queen Mother.

The canal became one of the most popular in Britain for pleasure boaters, but income from tolls always fell short of expenditure. British Waterways took back the southern section on 1 April 1988.

The bigger and deeper Warwick & Birmingham Canal, by contrast, was also hit hard by railway competition, but never became disused.

In 1917 the Warwick & Birmingham, Birmingham & Warwick Junction Canal and Warwick & Napton Canal companies became managed by one joint committee. In 1929 they were sold to the Regents Canal Company and became part of the new Grand Union Canal Company.

Huge sums of money were spent on converting the waterway from the top lock in Birmingham's Camp Hill to Regents Canal Dock in London into a broad canal, so that it could take boats up to 12 feet 6 inches wide, and creating a new trunk waterway.

Also nationalised in 1948, it too now has tourist traffic as its mainstay.

At Preston Bagot can be seen one of the distinctive split bridges on the Stratford-upon-Avon Canal, which allowed horses to switch from one side of the canal to the other without unhitching the rope from the barge they were pulling.

Autumnal reflections on the Stratford Canal in Illshaw Heath.

The drawbridge over the Stratford Canal at Major's Green near Shirley, which lends its name to the modern Drawbridge pub next door.

The wharf, a tiny 'branch' off the main canal, became known as Hockley Port, and the salt was stored in a warehouse next to the inn, which dates from 1868.

The Wharf Inn at Hockley Heath is a popular watering hole on the Stratford-upon-Avon Canal's northern section. Very much a modern village today, Hockley Heath was known in Saxon times as Hnuthyrste, meaning 'nut wood', referring to the forest. The name became transformed into Nuthurst: the church parish formed in its present state in 1878 is known as Nuthurst cum Hockley Heath.

The Bluebell cider house at Warings Green near Earlswood specialises in traditional cider.

11
TWIN BASTIONS OF POWER

Warwick and Kenilworth

Henley-in-Arden may well have been the capital of Arden, protected by the castle overlooking its twin town of Beaudesert.

However, the fortress was small beer in importance when compared to the mighty pair that lay to the east of the great woodland, Warwick Castle and Kenilworth Castle.

The county town of Warwick came into existence in late Saxon times, because of its strategic location on a small hill which became a fortress against Danish invaders.

Warwick was founded in 914 on the banks of the River Avon by Ethelfleda, sister of Edward the Elder, and daughter of the great Saxon monarch Alfred the Great. The name Warwick means 'dwellings by the weir.'

Warwick dominated not only the Avon valley but also the key crossing of the river on the roads to London, Stratford-upon-Avon and Coventry and the salt way to Droitwich.

The town, which overlooked earlier settlements, was protected by a wall and a ditch. However, they both proved ineffective in 1016, when the Danes finally invaded the town and burned it down, including the nunnery that stood on the site of the present-day St Nicholas church.

The fortifications nonetheless gave early Warwick vast importance as an administrative centre in the kingdom of Mercia, which included Arden. Then, as we saw in the first chapter, came Thurkill of Warwick, disloyal to King Harold but founder of the Arden 'dynasty.'

The eleventh century saw England carved up into administrative areas called shires, paving the way for the local government system we still have today.

The area controlled from Warwick became known as Warwickshire, and even before the Norman Conquest, the town had acquired the status of royal borough.

Warwick Castle as we know it today was built in two years as part of a national chain of fortifications so that William I could maintain power in his new and largely hostile kingdom.

In 1264, the castle came under attack from the forces of the sixth Earl of Leicester, Simon de Montfort, during the Second Barons' War of 1263–67 against his brother-in-law Henry III, with the defences being severely damaged.

Opposite: *The quintessential view of Warwick Castle as seen from the main road bridge over the Avon.*

Medieval armour aptly dominates Warwick Castle's Great Hall today.

Amongst many other deeds, de Montfort had argued the case for a parliament to advise the king, and many therefore consider him to be the founder of true British democracy. The king would not listen, and de Montfort later joined a group of barons who were opposed to the monarch's punitive taxes and eventually rebelled.

When the citizens of London tired of Henry, they invited de Montfort to take his place, but the king was having none of it, and moved his army against him.

De Montfort captured Henry during his victory at the Battle of Lewes in Sussex, and formed a government, but the king's son Prince Edward marched against him, and de Montfort was killed at the Battle of Evesham in 1265.

Afterwards, the castle and much of the town passed into the hands of the Beauchamp family, who became Earls of Warwick. They improved and strengthened the castle, adding its distinctive fourteenth-century towers, and surrounding the town with its protective walls, of which only the east and west gatehouses now remain.

Warwick is today one of the finest and most complete medieval castles in the country, inhabited continuously since the Middle Ages.

The Great Hall, the largest room in the castle, is its historic heart. Set against the wall is the magnificent Kenilworth buffet, made in oak by local craftsmen for the Great Exhibition of 1851.

The modern-day Kingmaker attraction inside the castle recreates the world of Richard Neville, Earl of Warwick, who was instrumental in deposing the weak Henry VI in 1461 and replacing him with Edward IV, before doing an about-turn and restoring Henry to the throne. For this, he earned the title Warwick the Kingmaker.

The most famous of all the castle's ghosts is Sir Fulke Greville, who haunts the Watergate Tower, now known as the Ghost Tower, after being brutally stabbed to death by his manservant in 1628.

Warwick was officially incorporated as a town in 1545, when Henry VIII established the King's New School of Warwick, although it had been functioning as an educational establishment since the days of Edward the Confessor.

During the English Civil War, Warwick was garrisoned for Parliament, and withstood a two-week siege from a 350-strong royalist army under the command of Colonel Purefoy between 1644 and 1646, and which failed to inflict as much damage to Warwick as the great fire of 1694 was to accomplish with far greater ease.

Much of the town centre was destroyed, including much of the medieval St Mary's church, although the chancel and the fifteenth-century Beauchamp chapel survive.

Warwick's East Gate, reconstructed in the early fifteenth century, when the chapel of St Peter was built above it. The arch spanned the original roadway.

The magnificent medieval Lord Leycester's Hospital adjoining Warwick's West Gate, with the Chapel of St James above it.

Warwick's Collegiate Church of St Mary, famous for its Beauchamp chapel, Norman crypt and medieval and Tudor tombs and tower.

However, the flames did not reach the town's magnificent half-timbered medieval Guildhall, which later became the Lord Leycester Hospital.

The gutted buildings were restored or replaced in seventeenth and early-eighteenth century styles, and today these form the core of the town centre, which thanks to planning protection has escaped the worst ravages of postwar 'modernisation' so blatant elsewhere, like Solihull for instance.

Yet while Warwick Castle has survived intact, its once-mighty Arden counterpart Kenilworth Castle, has been in ruins for the last 350 years.

Kenilworth Castle may have existed in the days of King Arthur, who was probably a Romano-British leader of the fifth or sixth century, by which time the Saxons had conquered Mercia. It may even have been an Arthurian stronghold.

Possibly demolished during the wars between King Edmund and the Danish King Canute, it was rebuilt a century later.

After the Norman Conquest, Kenilworth, a small settlement of about 100 villagers belonging to the royal manor of Stoneleigh, and whose history has been inextricably linked with that of the fortress it served, remained part of the king's estates until 1129 when Henry I gave it to his chamberlain and chief justice, Geoffrey de Clinton.

He replaced the basic Norman motte and bailey castle with a far grander affair befitting his lofty titles, with a deep outer moat and Caesar's Tower, a large keep. All that survives today of the first Norman castle is a ditch near the keep.

Under de Clinton, the castle became a much-feared and respected bastion of power, and eventually the concerned monarch demanded it back, considering it to have become far too

The half-timbered Tudor House Inn in West Street.

important for a subject to possess.

In 1244, Henry III appointed de Montfort as governor of the castle for life. De Montfort fortified the castle with all manner of military might – and then rebelled.

Following his abovementioned death at Evesham, many de Montfort supporters took shelter within the castle as the king's forces surrounded Kenilworth.

A stand-off led to the longest siege in English history, and proved that the castle, with its 20ft thick walls which could not be undermined, was so strong that it could withstand anything the king threw at it.

Siege engines proved useless, and Henry even ordered barges from Chester to be used in a bid to cross the defensive lake to gain access to the castle, but again in vain.

The defenders were defeated only by an epidemic worsened by famine, and they surrendered after nine months.

Edward I gave Kenilworth Castle to his youngest son Edmund, Earl of Lancaster, who was made Earl of Leicester.

Twenty-feet thick walls ensured that Kenilworth Castle once stood a nine-month siege. The castle reverts to its medieval name of Killingworth in Shakespeare's Henry VI Part 2.

Below: *The ruined keep of Kenilworth Castle, vandalism courtesy of Oliver Cromwell.*

Leicester's Gatehouse, which has been restored and houses an exhibition on the upper floors.

The castle was inherited by Edward II, who was later imprisoned in it by Henry, Earl of Lancaster, and later murdered at Berkeley Castle in Gloucestershire.

The castle eventually passed to John of Gaunt, Duke of Lancaster, the son of Edward III, and the most powerful man in the England of his day.

In 1364 John converted the fortress castle into a palace, enlarging it and adding domestic quarters and the Great Hall.

His grandson Henry V built a pleasure garden at the far end of the great lake, and lived at Kenilworth briefly after his landmark victory at Agincourt. Here according to tradition, he received the insulting French 'gift' of tennis balls which sparked off the Agincourt campaign, the subject of *Henry V*.

The castle was given by Queen Elizabeth I to Robert Dudley, Earl of Leicester, in 1563, and he turned it into a palace fit for her to visit, as she did on at least three occasions, the last being for 19 days in 1575. He added the towering mansion-sized Leicester's Building complete with a purpose-built 'dancing chamber.'

The last visit saw the most extravagant spectacle of pageantry that had in the history of England ever been laid on for the visit of a reigning monarch

The Parterre Garden at Kenilworth Castle.

Kenilworth Castle once offered views fit for a queen from these lofty windows.

When her majesty arrived, she was greeted by an "oracle" clad in white silk, and whose poetry told of the delight at her presence.

Passing through the first castle gate, Elizabeth was met by the legendary Lady of the Lake, attended by two nymphs also dressed in silk. The trio floated towards the queen from the centre of the mere on a moveable island, blazing with torches.

The sound of trumpets, drums and fifes, and the huge display of fireworks could be heard over the treetops 20 miles away. Disneyland had arrived four centuries early!

It has been claimed that the 11-year-old William Shakespeare was among the crowd . . . and that 20 years later, indelible memories of the occasion provided inspiration for his Ardenesque fairytale *A Midsummer Night's Dream*. After all, the castle had originally been built in a clearing in the great forest, just like the one in the play.

The castle changed hands twice during the English Civil War, without putting up too much resistance either time, its great medieval fortifications by now bypassed by military technology. However, Oliver Cromwell ordered parts of the walls and one side of the keep to be pulled down so it would cease forever to be a threat. The great lake was permanently drained to stop the castle from being used as a fort again.

The row of immaculate cottages on Kenilworth's Castle Green.

Charles II handed the castle to Sir Edward Hyde, who was appointed Baron Kenilworth and also Earl of Clarendon. Made famous by Walter Scott's romantic novel Kenilworth, published in 1821, the castle stayed in the Clarendon family until 1937 when it was bought by Sir John Siddeley, later Lord Kenilworth. The second Lord Kenilworth gave it to the town of *Kenilworth* in 1958 to mark the 400th anniversary of the coronation of Elizabeth I.

The ruins have been in the care of English Heritage since 1984, and the Tudor stables inside the castle wall survive intact. However, there are periodic calls to restore much more of the castle's former glory.

In 1988, when a public inquiry was held into bitterly-opposed plans to build a deep seam coal mine at Berkswell, one objection was that its workings would undermine the castle and prevent any future scheme to refill the great lake.

Today, you can view a copy of Dudley's last letter to Queen Elizabeth I, and explore his gatehouse where he courted his queen, following a multi-million pound investment which includes two exhibitions and the recreation of the original Elizabethan garden.

The great sandstone ruins of Kenilworth Castle, considered too mighty for one person to own.

12

MIDDLE ENGLAND

Meriden, Berkswell and Balsall Common

The village of Meriden is the traditional centre of England. The spot is said to be marked by the old market cross on the village green, near which stands a twentieth-century version, the Cyclists National Memorial, erected to the memory of cyclists who died in the two world wars.

Mathematicians, however, say that the exact centre of England is an unmarked point four miles to the south east of Atherstone.

So Meriden may not be at the precise axis of the country. Yet not so long ago, it governed the heart of England – not just its own parish, but a huge tract of old Warwickshire, stretching from near Atherstone in the north to Chadwick End near Knowle in the south, and from Marston Green in the west to the outskirts of Coventry in the east.

It was on 1 January 1895 that Meriden Rural District Council came into being, consisting of Meriden, Allesley, Berkswell, Bickenhill, Coleshill, Corley, Coundon, Fillongley, Hampton-in-Arden, Lea Marston, Sheldon, Shustoke, Nether Whitacre and Over Whitacre. However, regular local government changes nibbled away at it during the twentieth century, so while Meriden remains a parliamentary seat, the village and much of its former territory are now part of the Metropolitan Borough of Solihull.

Today, the 'Meriden Gap' of leafy Arden lanes and rolling pastureland separating the sprawling urban conurbations of Birmingham/Solihull and Coventry is under relentless pressures from developers.

In December 1964, the Government gave the go-ahead for Chelmsley Wood, an idyllic bluebell wood to the north of Marston Green, to be felled to make way for an overspill estate of 16,000 dwellings for Birmingham.

The failure of building such massive council estates to solve social deprivation was recognised by Solihull Council in 1989 when three Chelmsley Wood tower blocks, Grantley House, Pendrell House and Duntley House, were dynamited simultaneously.

Surely it would have been better to redevelop decaying parts of Birmingham in the first place, and leave the bluebell wood intact?

Above and opposite:
The medieval stone cross at Meriden on the village green, and a hand-coloured view from leafier times a century ago.

Thatched cottage overlooking Meriden's village green.

Meriden appeared around the fifteenth century as Miryden, a Saxon term meaning 'pleasant valley.' Before that, the village was known as Allespathe or Ailespede, meaning 'Aelli's way.'

Today it is home to England's oldest archery society, the Woodmen of Arden, who meet in the eighteenth-century Forest Hall.

Members shoot with the six-foot longbow used to great effect by Henry V's soldiers at Agincourt. The archery meetings in their present form were revived here in 1785.

The society claims that Robin Hood regularly won local archery tournaments.

At the Cyclists National Memorial, an annual festival of remembrance is held on the Sunday closest to 22 May. Yet Meriden is far better known for motorbikes than the pedal-powered variety, and for decades became a true centre of Britain – as far as the motorcycle industry was concerned.

For between 1942, when the business was moved from blitz-ravaged Coventry, and 1983, when it closed the village was home to the world-famous Triumph motorcycle factory, where world-beating machines were turned out. The factory has been replaced by a housing estate, with road names like Bonneville Close and Daytona Drive reflecting the site's heritage.

For many, the real gem of the 'Meriden Gap' is the village of Berkswell, which has made few concessions to the twenty-first century.

Berkswell originated as a clearing around a natural spring or well, a feature considered sacred by pre-Christian civilisations.

The area was ruled by a local warlord called Bercul, possibly a king of Mercia, said to have been baptised here by monks from Lichfield. Accordingly the place became known as Berculswell.

The well can still be seen today, the water rising near the entrance to the churchyard, and pouring into a square pit. Eventually it runs into the River Blythe, which forms the westernmost boundary of the Berkswell parish.

The church of St John the Baptist itself is magnificent, dating from Saxon times – some stonework from this period survives in the crypt – and has outstanding examples of Norman and Early English architecture. The building mainly dates from around 1150.

The Bear Inn is believed to be around four centuries old. It takes its name from the badge of Warwickshire, a bear and ragged staff, and has a Russian cannon at the front, captured during the Crimean War. During celebrations to mark the Golden Jubilee of Queen Victoria, it is said that the cannon was towed to the top of the nearest hill and fired – shattering many a Berkswell window.

The Cyclists National Memorial provides a twentieth-century equivalent.

A mid twentieth-century advertisement extolling the advantages of Meriden-built Triumph motorbikes.

A 1960s' advertisement for Triumph's lightweight single-cylinder Terrier motorbike – yours for £125 4s 6d!

Berkswell's superbly-preserved village well pictured a century ago and today. It supplied villagers until 1940.

Berkswell's splendid Norman parish church of St John the Baptist.

The village green still has its stocks and whipping post, highlighting medieval days when miscreants did not benefit from community service orders, probation or social workers.

Like Tanworth-in-Arden, Berkswell still has an Association for the Prosecution of Felons which predates the police force. It handed out rewards to citizens who arrested offenders. Catching a murderer was worth £20; a poacher taken in daylight was worth just ten shillings, but £1 if he was detained at night.

The village reading room, now the village hall, dates from 1902. A curate who may have been a nephew of the novelist George Eliot organised readings there.

Maud Watson, daughter of rector the Reverend Dr Watson, won the first ladies lawn tennis championship at Wimbledon in 1884, and became the founding president of Berkswell's Women's Institute.

Three other Berkswell women made national headlines before the First World War, as suffragettes. They were jailed after taking stones from Berkswell to hurl through the windows of 10 Downing Street.

Preserved Berkswell Windmill in Windmill Lane, Balsall Common is a splendid example of a Warwickshire brick tower mill, built in 1826 on the site of an earlier post mill.

The machinery was powered by wind until 1927, when a mechanical engine was installed. It ceased operations in 1948, and restored twice afterwards, still has its sails and all its internal machinery.

Balsall Common itself has become a sizeable modern commuter settlement largely dating from the 1950s and with a population of 12,000, but it too retains some medieval features, not least of all the thirteenth-century half-timbered Saracens Head pub, which was there at the time when the Knights Templar at nearby Temple Balsall were concerning themselves with the Crusades.

Early nineteenth-century stagecoaches running between Stratford-upon-Avon and Coleshill raced through Balsall Common along Kenilworth Road. Horses were changed at the Shay House, an old brick dwelling on the left before the George in the Tree pub, where in earlier times cattle drovers from North Wales stopped en route to London.

Another local pub acquired worldwide fame through a conflict many centuries after the Crusades.

In 1904, a young disabled boy, Harry Williams, who spent most of his childhood studying music, moved with his family to the Plough Inn at Meer End.

There, he wrote songs, including one published in 1912 called *It's A Long Way to Tipperary*.

It became a popular marching song during the First World War, and Harry became so wealthy through songwriting royalties that he bought the pub outright for his parents.

Harry died there in 1924 and was buried alongside his parents in Temple Balsall. The pub became known as the Tipperary Inn in honour of the song.

A school has existed in Berkswell since at least 1500. The present one has always been run by the Church of England.

The Saracens Head pub was there when local warrior monks fought Crusades in the Holy Land.

Law enforcement in old Arden: the village stocks at Berkswell village green.

It's not a long way to the Tipperary Inn from Balsall Common, just a mile down the road at Meer End.

Berkswell Windmill, in which medieval wind technology was honed to perfection.

Sare Hole, near Moseley.

418.

13
TOLKIEN'S ARDEN

Sarehole, Hall Green, Moseley Bog and the River Cole

Birmingham has been called the workshop of the world, for its historical excellence in manufacturing. Yet despite the intensive urbanisation that inevitably accompanies centuries of industrial prowess, it is surprising to find it is still a very 'green' city.

If you look over the city skyline from vantage points, one of the most distinctive features is a green 'canopy' created by the high number of mature trees in parks, along roadways and in inner-city back gardens.

Arden covered much of Birmingham, and while the city swallowed up much of its green acres with rapid expansion in the decades following the First World War, the old forest has not yielded its territory easily.

Taking pride of place amongst leafier suburbs is Hall Green and its old hamlet of Sarehole, a place which has had an impact of Shakespearean proportions on world literature.

For it was here that John Ronald Reuel Tolkien (1892–1973) lived between the age of four and eight, and drew upon the rural backwater a stone's throw from his family's home at 264 Wake Green Road for the great Gothic landscapes of *The Hobbit* and *The Lord of the Rings*.

Tolkien, who was born in Blomfontein in Orange Free State, moved with his mother Mabel and brother Hilary to Sarehole after his father Arthur died in South Africa from rheumatic fever. He spent much of his formative years immersing himself in his surroundings, and later lived in Edgbaston, where the Victorian tower of Edgbaston Waterworks and the similarly lofty Perrott's Tower may have influenced the dark towers in his works.

That watermill from which Bilbo Baggins and his dwarf companions hid in barrels to flee the Elves comes straight from Sarehole Mill, a Grade II listed building on the River Cole, which dates from 1542.

The existing building, now a free museum, was constructed in 1771 and later hired by steam technology pioneer Matthew Boulton for scientific experiments, converting the flour-milling machinery for metal working.

Opposite: *Sarehole Mill as Tolkien would have known it. Today's busy Cole Bank Road crosses the ford by a bridge and carries the No 11 Outer Circle bus route.*

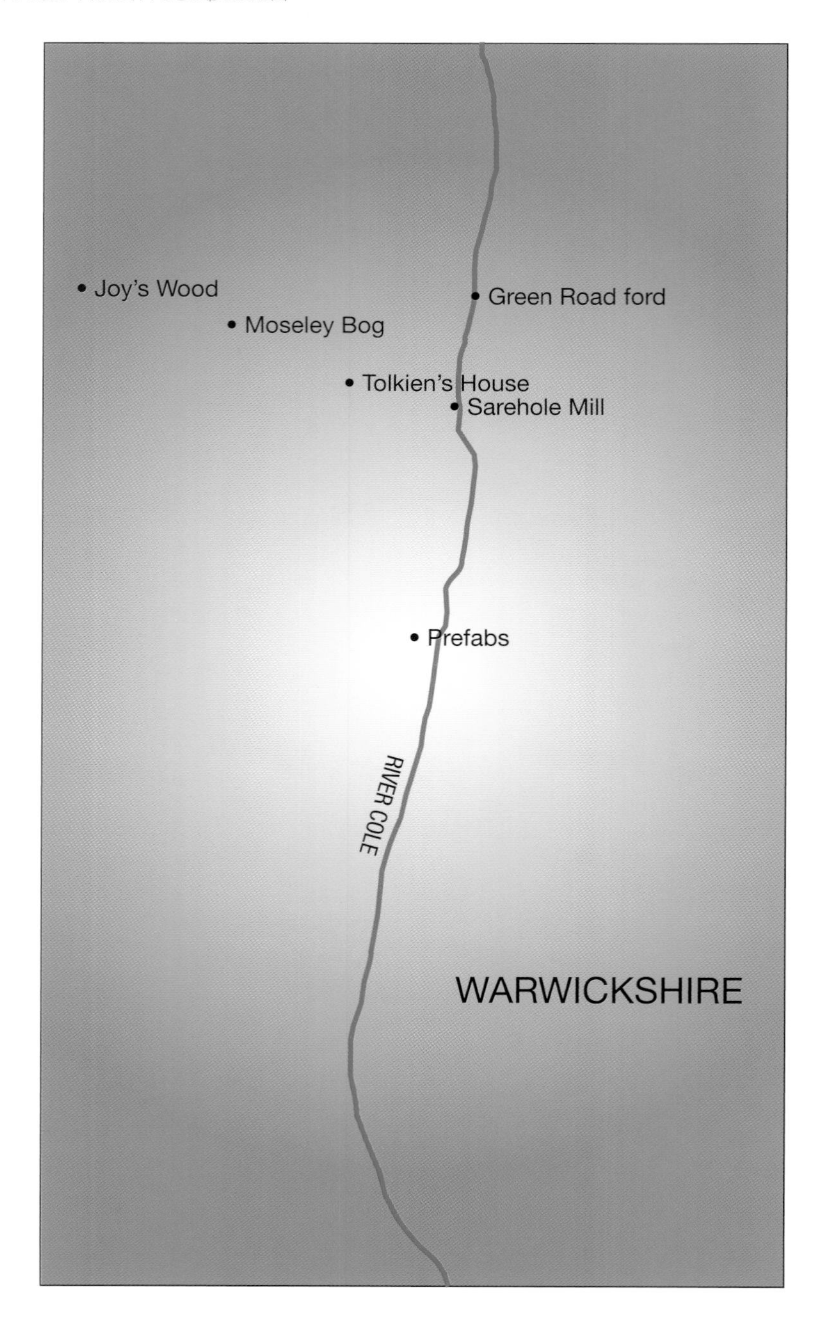
Joy's Wood
Moseley Bog
Green Road ford
Tolkien's House
Sarehole Mill
Prefabs
RIVER COLE
WARWICKSHIRE

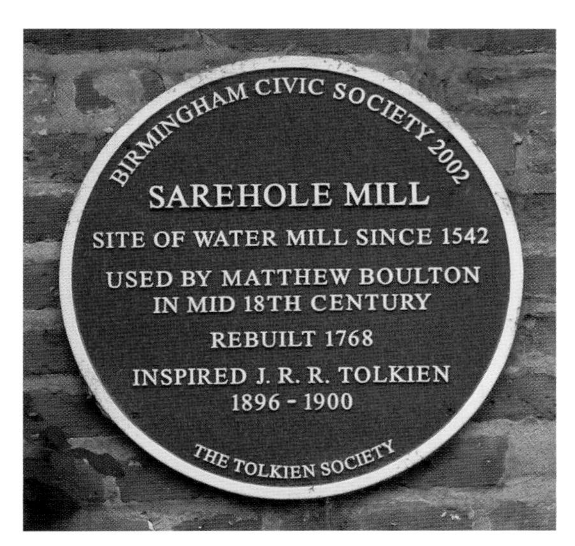

One of the millstones.

The mill machinery is preserved intact.

An autumnal view from across Sarehole millpond.

The first edition of The Hobbit.

Tolkien's Sarehole has a long way to go before it succumbs to the commercial exploitation that long ago beset Shakespeare's Stratford – but the Hungry Hobbit café in Wake Green Road is a start!

Three years before Sarehole Mill was restored in 1969, Tolkien confirmed he had used it in his book: "*It was a kind of lost paradise . . . There was an old mill that really did grind corn with two millers, a great big pond with swans on it, a sandpit, a wonderful dell with flowers, a few old-fashioned village houses and, further away, a stream with another mill. I always knew it would go – and it did.*"

Sarehole – the name means 'water meadow' – influenced his creation of the green and peaceful Shire where hobbits lived in harmony.

Nearby Moseley Bog, a now-drained secondary reservoir of Sarehole millpond and a unique wetland wildlife habitat, was a likely setting for the Old Forest, haunt of Treebeard and his fellow Ents.

A legend that the hill on which Spring Hill Cottage stands is riddled with secret tunnels could have inspired Tolkien's 'Bag End'.

Saved from development by a vociferous local campaign, Moseley Bog hosted the first-ever International Dawn Chorus Day in 1984. The event is held on the first Sunday in May, encouraging people to rise early to listen to birdsong.

The Cole, first recorded in 849, takes its name from the Celtic for 'hazel'. It has also been given the title of Little Niagara because of spectacular floods.

The source of the Cole is at Red Hill near Kings Norton, 600 feet above sea level.

It is known as Inkford Brook as it crosses the boundary between Worcestershire and Warwickshire, and Saddlers Brook as it passes the Arden hamlet of Tanners Green where leatherware was once made using vast quantities of Cole water.

Another important medieval trade was the cultivation of willow trees for withy to make baskets, and the presence of water was also a prime consideration. A settlement known as Withthan or Withworth because of its withies grew up, the name being transferred to the modern commuter village of Wythall a mile to the north.

Wake Green Road near Tolkien's home, still lined with trees today.

The Cole makes a U-turn from its original southerly direction to run north into Shirley and Birmingham, where it provides a green lung with stretches of public open space like Trittiford Park and a riverside walk through the postwar suburban sprawl.

Beyond Hall Green, the Cole enters areas where industrialisation has not been so kind to its banks. However, much of the valley north of Hay Mills became recreation grounds like Heybarnes, Newbridge Farm and Batchelors Farm, and stayed 'green'.

The Cole eventually reaches its own town, Coleshill, and a mile past the appropriately-named Cole End, is absorbed by the Blythe, shortly before that river joins the Tame, and Arden reaches its northernmost limit.

Joy's Wood, the entrance to Moseley Bog, and possibly Tolkien's Old Forest.

The sylvan River Cole alongside Sarehole Mill.

Moseley Bog, much loved by Tolkien, with the Coldbath Brook running through the middle to Sarehole Mill.

The striking landmark church of St Mary, Wythall, designed by Frederick Preedy of London, dates from 1862, but is no longer used for worship.

These idyllic scenes of a cottage and ford across the Cole in Green Road, Hall Green could so easily fit any of the classic Arden villages in this book, yet are less than four miles from the centre of Britain's second city. Gravel deposits laid down in the Ice Age allow the Cole to be forded in many places.

Preserved prefabs in Wake Green Road. Grade II listed, they are the last survivors of hundreds made from factory-built components and bolted together on site, providing instant homes for Birmingham families whose homes were destroyed in the Nazi blitz. Many residents preferred their temporary homes to the houses they had lost, and stayed in them permanently.

This ancient oak in the appropriately-named Arden Road in Acocks Green has a traffic island all to itself, but has been heavily pruned for safety reasons.

THE SHAKESPEARE EXPRESS
4965

14
STEAMING BACK THROUGH ARDEN

The 'Shakespeare Express'

At the start of our discovery of Arden, we saw a dense canopy of trees stretching across central and northern Warwickshire.

Over the centuries, its ancient trackways became green lanes and medieval highways as more and more clearings appeared, followed by stagecoach routes.

However, railways opened up Arden to mass transport like nothing that had gone before.

The London & Birmingham Railway via Coventry and Balsall Common (now the electrified West Coast Main Line from Euston) opened in 1838.

The Great Western Railway reached Birmingham from Paddington via Warwick and Solihull in 1852, and developed a grand through terminus at Snow Hill.

Stratford-upon-Avon was reached firstly by the Oxford, Worcester & Wolverhampton Railway from the south in 1859. A GWR route from Hatton Junction on the London line via Bearley arrived in 1860.

A line from Barnt Green to Alcester run by the Midland Railway was completed by 1866 (and closed in 1963).

A line from Fenny Compton to Stratford (reached 1873) and Broom Junction on the Alcester line (reached 1879), later known as the Stratford-Upon-Avon & Midland Junction Railway, gave the town a second station, which closed to passengers completely by 1952.

Shorter branches appeared, like that from Rowington Junction to Henley-in-Arden and Bearley to Alcester which have already been described.

The last major line built was the GWR's North Warwickshire Line from Tyseley in Birmingham to Bearley, where it joined the route to Stratford. Built as double track and opened in 1908, it became part of a main line from Birmingham to the west of England.

Motor transport took its toll on railways. The final passenger trains to Stratford from the south ran in 1969, freight ending seven years later before the line was ripped up.

Miraculously, the North Warwickshire Line survived several post-Beeching attempts at closure or truncation, and is now a major commuter route. In a country where the national network no

The nameplate of Rood Ashton Hall, which was bought by Birmingham Railway Museum from Barry scrapyard in South Wales in the mistaken belief that it was sister locomotive No 4983 Albert Hall. It was only when the restoration of the rusting hulk to main line running standard reached an advanced stage that the true identity was discovered.

Opposite:
Restored to original glory, Rood Ashton Hall heads a 'Shakespeare Express' from Stratford via Hatton Junction.

longer, at the time of writing, runs passenger trains to substantial towns like Corby and Leek, it is wonderful to find daily services still calling at places like Earlswood Lakes, Wood End, Danzey and Wootton Wawen.

One of the best ways to appreciate the full richness of the Arden countryside is from the elevated heights of a train.

Under the banner of Vintage Trains, Birmingham Railway Museum successfully runs two round 'Shakespeare Express' trips from the city to Stratford and back on summer Sundays, using GWR locomotives restored to pristine condition. The outward journey runs via Shirley, and the return via Solihull. Bookings can be made on 0121 708 4960.

The coat of arms of the Great Western Railway, which had two routes running from Birmingham through the heart of old Arden.

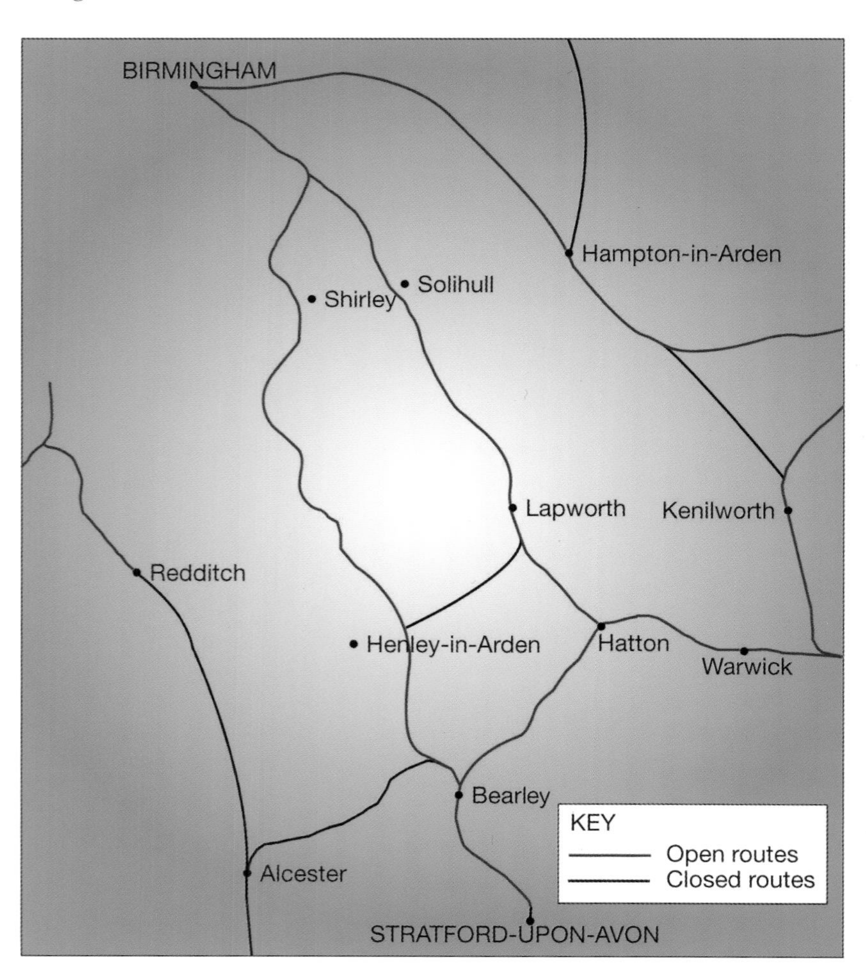